The
WELL-
BALANCED
TEACHER

The
WELL-
BALANCED
TEACHER

How to Work Smarter and Stay Sane
Inside the Classroom and Out

ASCD

Alexandria, Virginia USA

1703 N. Beauregard St. • Alexandria, VA 22311–1714 USA
Phone: 800-933-2723 or 703-578-9600 • Fax: 703-575-5400
Web site: www.ascd.org • E-mail: member@ascd.org
Author guidelines: www.ascd.org/write

Gene R. Carter, *Executive Director;* Judy Zimny, *Chief Program Development Officer;* Nancy Modrak, *Publisher;* Scott Willis, *Director, Book Acquisitions & Development;* Julie Houtz, *Director, Book Editing & Production;* Leah Lakins, *Editor;* Catherine Guyer, *Senior Graphic Designer;* Mike Kalyan, *Production Manager;* Valerie Younkin, *Typesetter;* Sarah Plumb, *Production Specialist*

Printed in the United States of America. Cover art © 2010 by ASCD. ASCD publications present a variety of viewpoints. The views expressed or implied in this book should not be interpreted as official positions of the Association.

All Web links in this book are correct as of the publication date below but may have become inactive or otherwise modified since that time. If you notice a deactivated or changed link, please e-mail books@ascd.org with the words "Link Update" in the subject line. In your message, please specify the Web link, the book title, and the page number on which the link appears.

PAPERBACK ISBN: 978-1-4166-1069-4   ASCD product #111004   n9/10

Also available as an e-book (see Books in Print for the ISBNs).

Quantity discounts for the paperback edition only: 10–49 copies, 10%; 50+ copies, 15%; for 1,000 or more copies, call 800-933-2723, ext. 5634, or 703-575-5634. For desk copies: member@ascd.org.

Library of Congress Cataloging-in-Publication Data
Anderson, Mike.
    The well-balanced teacher : how to work smarter and stay sane inside the classroom and out / Mike Anderson.
        p. cm.
    Includes bibliographical references and index.
    ISBN 978-1-4166-1069-4 (pbk. : alk. paper)   1. Effective teaching.   2. Educational innovations.
3. School improvement programs.   4. Learning, Psychology of. I. Title.
    LB1025.3.M536 2010
    371.1—dc22
                                                                                2010021125

20 19 18 17 16 15 14 13 12 11 10   1 2 3 4 5 6 7 8 9 10 11 12

*For Ethan, Carly, and children everywhere
who deserve nothing less than teachers who are healthy,
happy, and passionate about teaching and learning.*

The Well-Balanced Teacher

How to Work Smarter and Stay Sane Inside the Classroom and Out

Acknowledgments

For years, I have argued that writing prompts on standardized tests are a terrible way to assess good writing. Writers don't sit down and compose final drafts in one sitting, unable to communicate with other people. It is much more dynamic and interactive than that. I cannot imagine trying to write without sharing ideas, asking for advice, and being pushed and helped by others. Writing this book has only strengthened my view that writing is truly a collaborative process. So, here is an attempt to include many of the people who helped in the writing of this book.

Thanks so much to the many teachers in Portsmouth, New Hampshire who helped me research and formulate much of my initial thinking and attempts at writing on this subject. Jenn Dunham, you were especially helpful for the countless hours you put up with me as I babbled on and on at lunches, before school, after school, and every other time I could pin you down. Pat Ganz, I appreciate your input, ideas, and long conversations!

Thanks so much to my dedicated and joyful team of colleagues at Northeast Foundation for Children who encouraged me throughout this process and who helped me talk through second (and third, and fourth, and...) drafts. Babs Freeman-Loftis, Margaret Berry Wilson, Kerry O'Grady, Tina Valentine, Andy Dousis, Paula Denton, Alice Yang, Mary Beth Forton, and so many others. You rock!

Thanks so much to all of the teachers around the country who graciously gave up lunch breaks and spare time at conferences and workshops to think about, talk about, and share your questions, ideas, and challenges about staying healthy and balanced in our profession.

Thanks also to the team at ASCD who were willing to take this project on and make it better and better through each step of the process.

Thanks to my mother, Susan Trask, and my father, Marion Anderson, for passing along a love of teaching and learning, and for many conversations about balancing life and work.

Margaret Berry Wilson, colleague, fellow writer, and friend, also deserves a special thanks. She selflessly gave hours of her time, reading and rereading this entire book, pushing me to be clearer, challenging me to answer new questions and consider different perspectives, and warning me to tone things down from time to time. Because of her skillful questions, respectful disagreements, and genuine encouragement, this book is better.

Most importantly, I want to thank my wife, Heather, and my children, Ethan and Carly, who provide me with the best reasons to stay healthy and balanced!

Foreword

By Linda Lantieri

It happened in an instant. A teaching challenge more difficult than any curriculum planner could possibly imagine, a student task too daunting for even the most capable child, an unplanned assessment that nobody would ever require: 5,000 school children and 200 teachers engulfed in a black cloud of dust, running for their lives. It was the morning of September 11, 2001, and there they were, students and teachers holding hands, fleeing to safety, singing chants and rhymes to take their minds off the horror. This unimaginable event included the sight of office workers jumping from the Twin Towers of the World Trade Center, a spectacle which, in an impossible moment of improvisation, some children re-imagined as birds and butterflies falling from the windows.

Thankfully, every teacher and student in Lower Manhattan survived the events of September 11th. Many educators, particularly the first-hand witnesses on that fateful day, were left asking a fundamental question about the purpose and goal of education—Can we cultivate or teach the ways of being that helped teachers and students at Ground Zero maintain calm and balance in the face of profound stress and uncertainty? Moreover, beyond September 11th, can we teach the habits of mind, body, and heart that will prepare us for the numerous uncertainties that are part of answering the call to teach?

Since September 11th, I have a much deeper respect for the important work of supporting teachers to maintain their balance. It became clear that the teachers in Lower Manhattan needed to first build their own reservoir of inner resilience. They had to develop that place inside themselves that gives their work meaning and purpose **before** we could expect them to offer it to their colleagues or students.

The events surrounding September 11th became an opportunity to acknowledge that teachers have an inner life. It became evident that their inner lives required nurturing so that they could provide the healing their students so desperately needed. This tragedy also provided an opening to acknowledge how deeply educators need to be equipped with better stress management and coping skills. Teaching is one of the most stressful professions there is. As I offered my help to teachers in and around Ground Zero, I became more aware that when teachers get in touch with their own inner balance, it becomes easier for them to align who they are on the inside with who they are on the outside. When teachers can have this kind of balance within the context of a community of learners, they will have the potential to allow their personal growth to be a source of social change and mutual inspiration. The irony is that those teachers I worked with in schools at Ground Zero needed what we had to give them on September 10, 2001. We don't have to wait for another tragedy for teachers to learn how to balance themselves. This is the potential that Mike Anderson offers us in his book, *The Well-Balanced Teacher*.

As the modern stresses of today's "ordinary" teaching and learning accumulate, Mike helps us to ask how we can become more well-balanced so that we can connect to our deep inner strength and resilience, avoid burnout, and actually enjoy the journey of being a classroom teacher. That is a tall order! Yet the benefits of being well-balanced teachers, as Mike points out, are enormous. Teachers who learn to balance their inner and outer lives are able to better regulate their emotional reactivity and reduce emotional exhaustion and burnout. Aware and responsive teachers can manage their classrooms well because they are proactive rather than reactive. They notice what is going on around them. How can we help teachers remember to put themselves on their own best friend list so they can enjoy teaching, love their students, and stay whole in the process?

The Well-Balanced Teacher answers this question. This book is an exquisite blend of research and first-hand experience, bridging both the scientific and subjective worlds. Mike offers simple yet practical strategies for effectively dealing with the balancing act that real-life teachers face. His own personal vignettes, as well as those of others, offer realistic hope and comfort in terms of what is possible. He gives us resourceful ways to lessen the tension between expectations of the profession and the inner and outer resources one can cultivate. *The Well-Balanced Teacher* is a valuable resource for any teacher faced with figuring out how to become stress hardy *and* fulfilled in answering the courageous call to teach. Through his personal experiences as a teacher, his conversations with his colleagues, and his research on stress, Mike offers us a roadmap for a teaching career that can be life giving for both ourselves and those we love.

In the end, it is clear that it is up to us to reframe our role as teachers in a way that gives it the meaning and significance we want it to have in our lives. We have to remember how to balance everything else that is also important—including ourselves. Our growth as teachers is often not supported by our school systems, so it is up to us to find that balance. *The Well-Balanced Teacher* provides wise guidance for creating lives that are more resonant with how we really want to be, both in the classroom and out. When I was asked to write the foreword to this book, I jumped at the chance. ASCD's whole child initiative talks about ensuring that each child is healthy, safe, engaged, supported, **and** challenged. In fact these are the exact same characteristics teachers would like to use to describe what they need as well. I am delighted by the thought of how many teachers' lives will benefit from this practical wisdom.

Linda Lantieri, MA, currently serves as the director of *The Inner Resilience Program*. This program equips school personnel with the skills and strategies to strengthen their inner lives in order to model these skills for the young people in their care. Linda is also one of the founding board members of the Collaborative for Academic, Social, and Emotional Learning (CASEL). She has over 40 years of experience in education as a former teacher and director of a middle school in East Harlem and as a faculty member at Hunter College in New York City. Linda is the co-author of *Waging Peace in Our Schools* (Beacon

Press, 1996) editor of *Schools with Spirit: Nurturing the Inner Lives of Children and Teachers* (Beacon Press, 2001), and author of *Building Emotional Intelligence: Techniques to Cultivate Inner Strength in Children* (Sounds True, 2008). She can be reached by e-mail at llantieri@att.net.

Preface

There's no doubt that teaching is a tough profession, and it doesn't seem to be getting any easier. Teachers manage an incredible array of roles and responsibilities including planning and teaching lessons, communicating with parents, collaborating with colleagues, and staying current on educational trends and new legal policies. From No Child Left Behind to peanut-free cafeteria tables to professional learning communities to arts and technology in the classroom, teachers have a lot of responsibilities to juggle. Whether good or bad, these new trends seem to be accelerating at an alarming rate and show no signs of slowing down.

Challenged with an increasingly complicated and sometimes overwhelming career, too many teachers seem to end up in one of two extreme places. Some teachers overwork themselves. They spend weekends at school, lug tote bags full of papers home each night, and become physically, mentally, and emotionally exhausted. Some teachers end up taking doctor-ordered leaves of absences for stress-related illnesses and fatigue. Other teachers take the reverse course: they disconnect. They skip staff meetings and professional development sessions, teach the same uninspired lessons and units year after year, and beat the bus out of the parking lot each afternoon.

A few teachers, though, have struck a happy medium. Passionate and visionary teachers pour their hearts and souls into their students and their schools, but they don't become overwhelmed with work and stress. They manage to sing in a choir or run 10K road races on the weekends. They hike with friends and garden. Not surprisingly, the best teachers I have ever seen fall into this category. They are positive with their students, parents, and colleagues. They are innovative and motivated to improve their practice. They are willing to take risks and try new ideas.

As a teacher, I wanted to know more about how to do that myself.

Thus began many years of research that prompted the writing of this book. I collected information and ideas from a variety of sources. First and foremost, I had my own experiences as a classroom teacher. I began to notice and record times when I was most stressed out and when I felt healthiest. I started looking for connections between the way I took care of myself and the energy I had for my students. Another valuable resource was the group of colleagues in my school. I developed many ongoing conversations with colleagues about how to stay healthy and vibrant in the classroom. I also talked with teachers from around the country, first as a part-time consulting teacher who taught summer workshops, and then as a full-time consulting teacher for a nonprofit organization. I interviewed hundreds of teachers in a variety of schools and settings. Finally, I poured through educational journals and books about teacher stress and health. What began as my own personal struggle to find balance and sanity in my own teaching has evolved into this compilation of insights and strategies that I offer to you in this book.

As I began to work more and more with the ideas in this book, several categories emerged that encapsulated the main struggles most of us face when attempting to stay healthy, balanced, and professionally passionate. Each category evolved into its own chapter. They are as follows:

• **Meeting our most basic needs.** If we're going to be effective caregivers, we must first care for our own most basic needs: healthy food, hydration, sleep, exercise, and emotional and spiritual refreshment.

• **Belonging.** We need to feel positive connections with other people, both in school (students, colleagues, administrators, and parents) and outside of school (family and friends).

• **Significance.** We need to know that we make a positive difference through the work we do. We need to maintain a healthy perspective about our roles and impact on our schools.

• **Positive engagement.** When we enjoy what we do, we have great energy and passion for our work. When something doesn't go well, we can recover and rebound more quickly.

• **Balance.** Healthy teachers set boundaries and create healthy routines so that their work is meaningful, rich, and energetic, and they can also have healthy lives outside of their classrooms and schools.

So, here's the driving force that runs through this whole book—we **must** learn to take better care of ourselves so that we can take better care of others. And though many of us may already *know* this deep down inside, actually *doing something about it* can be challenging. So, instead of shoving our own personal needs into the background, let's start addressing them head on. We must begin to view taking care of ourselves not as a selfish pursuit to tackle once our work is done, but as an integral part of our daily work as teachers. Our students deserve no less!

CHAPTER 1

The Importance of Managing Stress

About 10 years ago, I had a revelation—I could not do everything that I was being asked to do in the classroom. This was only part of the revelation, though. At this point, I had been a teacher for six years. The full revelation was not just that I could not get everything done that I was being asked to do, but that I *still* could not do it. My first few years, I had assumed that my inability to complete all of the teaching I was supposed to do was mostly due to inexperience and that one day I would have it all figured out. I had this vague vision of myself feeling relaxed and confident as I delivered perfectly timed lessons and units, one flowing into the next in a seamless transition that had me finishing all curricula in the middle of June. Not only was I nowhere near this vision after six years of teaching, but I actually seemed to be farther from it than I had been a few years before. Instead of getting closer to that magical, mystical place where I had time to teach and time to relax, I seemed more hopelessly swamped than ever. I was working harder, putting in more time and energy than ever before, but still having to sift through the remaining content I had not yet reached each April, deciding what not to teach.

I decided to do a little information collecting. For one whole year, I tracked every minute that was taken away from my teaching. I kept a very simple log on the computer, and every time we had a fire drill, a visit from Officer

Friendly, a half-day for professional development, or any other interruption that took time away from my time with students, I recorded the date, the activity, and the time lost. I made no attempt to judge whether I felt the time lost was valuable or a waste of time. In fact, quite a few of the activities, such as our artist-in-residence program, were quite valuable, and I would hate to lose them. I simply wanted to track how much time I really had to teach. Figure 1.1 shows what I found.

Figure 1.1	Total Time Lost: 1999–2000 School Year	
Activities	**Total Minutes**	**Number of 4.5-Hour Instructional Days**
Band	1,260	4.67
Chorus	1,640	6.074
Literacy PD	310	1.146
Early release for professional development	600	2.22
Early release for holidays	600	2.22
Morning announcements	900	3.27
PM safety patrol	900	3.27
Delayed openings (snow)	600	2.22
All-school meetings	125	0.4628
Other assemblies	440	1.629
Guest speakers	170	0.63
Fire drills/lock-down drills/bus safety	41	0.15
Artist-in-residence	65	0.407
Nurse visits (scoliosis, hearing, etc.)	15	0.06
State testing	255	0.94
End-of-year trips and activities	720	2.67
Meetings/trainings	320	1.184
School pictures	30	0.12
Book fair preview	30	0.12
Total	9,021	33.41

During that year, children in Portsmouth, New Hampshire had a six-hour school day. Each day, students had 45 minutes for lunch and recess and 45 minutes for special classes, such as physical education, art, music, computer, and library time. After that time was spent, teachers had 4.5 hours available for classroom instruction. In our school, we were expected to spend one hour a day reading, one hour a day working on math, 45 minutes a day writing, about 20 minutes a day running a morning meeting, 15 minutes a day working on word study, and 15 minutes a day reading aloud. These times were stated verbally or in writing by either administration or our literacy team. Forty-five minutes a day for science and social studies would have given us a chance of getting in all of our teaching objectives, though few 5th grade teachers taught both science and social studies at any one time.

When you add up all of these times, you get a total of five hours and five minutes a day. Already we see a problem: a deficit of 35 minutes a day. Figure 1.2 illustrates this time challenge. When you consider all of the time lost to chorus practice, guest speakers, and other activities, we actually had an average of 3 hours and 40 minutes per day of teaching time. And this was before the No Child Left Behind (NCLB) act hit the fan and tripled the amount of time spent on testing.

Figure 1.2	Real Time to Teach
Time to Teach	**Explanation**
5 hours and 5 minutes	This is the total expected instructional time when all of the separate expectations (e.g., 60 minutes for reading or 60 minutes for math) were combined.
4 hours and 30 minutes	This is the amount of teaching time in a normal school day (a 6-hour day minus 45 minutes for lunch/recess and specials).
3 hours and 40 minutes	This is the average amount of instructional time we actually had when all interruptions were factored in.

Have you noticed the total at the end of Figure 1.1? Over one-sixth of the school year's instructional time was actually spent on other activities. Again, some of these activities are valuable and should not be removed, but it is important to consider that as these various activities divert our class time to other places, the amount of curriculum that we are expected to teach rarely decreases. Something else important to recognize about these numbers is that they only reflect the impossibility of actually delivering the amount of instruction we are supposed to. These data do not track the planning and record keeping required for this amount of instruction or the other tasks that teachers have in addition to planning and teaching, which grew significantly during my first six years in the classroom.

On the one hand, these results might seem disheartening, but at the time I collected them, they actually had the reverse effect on me. I was positively elated. It was not my fault! My inability to catch up and teach everything was not just a series of personal defects accumulating in failure. I was, in fact, being asked to do the impossible.

On the other hand, having the information did not do much to alleviate the problem. I still had too much to do, too much to teach, and too many other responsibilities—and that problem was not going away, either. Other than forwarding my research results to my principal and my superintendent, who responded with a polite if somewhat bland "thanks for the information" type of response, there was not much that I could do to lessen my workload and stress. Or was there?

Research on Stress and Teaching

Teaching is one of the most stressful professions. I have always believed this. But then again, I might be biased. My mother was a 3rd grade teacher for 19 years before becoming a literacy consultant and mentor teacher in her district. My father was a college professor for 37 years. His father was an elementary school administrator. I taught at the elementary level for 15 years and have worked with other teachers throughout the country as a consulting teacher for many years. My wife, Heather, taught 2nd grade for seven years before staying home full-time with our two children. Our very good friends and neighbors across the street teach 5th grade and kindergarten. Many of my other good friends are teachers, too. I have always been surrounded by teachers.

I have other friends and family who are not teachers, and their careers and lives are also stressful. When I talk with them about the difficulties and stresses of teaching, I get a mix of sympathy and "Oh, give me a break—every job is stressful" looks. So I began to wonder: is teaching really more stressful than most professions, or does it just seem that way to someone who is a teacher and is surrounded by teachers?

As it turns out, teaching *is* one of the most stressful professions. In study after study on workplace stress that I analyzed, teaching came out at or near the top in nearly every one. Try this: Google "most stressful jobs" and look at what comes up. At the time of this writing, nearly every entry cited teaching as one of the top 10 most stressful professions. Some recent studies are particularly interesting.

A study done in the UK reports that 41 percent of teachers have high levels of stress at work (Baker, 2004). This figure was *double* the average amount of occupational stress reported in the rest of the survey group. The next two highest groups reporting extreme workplace stress were nurses and managers (Baker, 2004), which is interesting because many teachers frequently find themselves in these roles on a frequent basis in the classroom. A recent study of special educators in Greece found extremely high levels of stress among this group, citing emotional burnout, heavy workloads, challenging collegial relationships, and many other factors that contribute to high teacher stress (Antoniou, Polychroni, & Walters, 2000). In a study focused on teachers in the Midwest, 40 percent of teachers reported high levels of stress, while only 12 percent reported low or very low levels of stress (Block, 2003). The National Association of Head Teachers conducted a survey of their own and found that 40 percent of head teachers reported visiting a doctor with a stress-related problem during the previous year. According to the Web site of the Centers for Disease Control and Prevention (2006), inner-city high school teachers are more likely to get an ulcer than any other professionals.

I could go on, but I am preaching to the choir. You don't need any convincing that teaching is stressful. Now we need to ask, So what?

So What?

Okay, teaching is stressful. You might say that it has always been stressful, so what's the big deal? Stress is a part of the job, and we should all just suck it up and stop whining, right? Wrong!

The Cost of Stress

There are multiple reasons why we should care about our emotional selves. Workers who report high levels of stress have 46 percent higher annual health costs (Ingebretsen, 2005). Teachers who are stressed out also take more sick days and are less productive when they are at school (Van Der Linde, 2000). These conditions cost school districts enormous amounts of money. In addition, multiple physical ailments come with repeatedly high doses of stress. In the short term, people have fight-or-flight physical responses when under stress: increased heart rate, quicker breathing, sweating, a rise in blood sugar, and greater muscular tension are just a few. Long-term effects of stress "can lead to serious health problems. Chronic stress disrupts nearly every system in your body. It can raise blood pressure, suppress the immune system, increase the risk of heart attack and stroke, contribute to infertility, and speed up the aging process. Long-term stress can even rewire the brain, leaving you more vulnerable to anxiety and depression" (Smith, Jaffe-Gill, & Segal, 2009).

These conditions can be enormously costly for us and our school districts. Let's do a little simple math as an illustration. What if every professional in a school district needed to take just one sick day a year because of stress-related issues? Imagine a moderately sized district with about 1,000 professional staff members. Substitute teachers are paid about $75 a day, so one stress-related sick day for everyone would cost the district $75,000. This figure is roughly the equivalent of two new teachers' salaries in many places. And that is only for one sick day each!

Our Friends and Families

More important than the actual monetary cost of illness and stress is the damage that can be done to our personal relationships. When we are overburdened with work, it can be hard to make enough time to spend with our friends and family. When our stress level is high, we may not be able to give them the full attention they deserve, or our mood may sour to the point where people don't enjoy our company. If we allow our personal relationships to slip, it becomes even easier to retreat into our work, and the problem worsens. The added stress of strained personal relationships of course has a negative impact on our ability to be joyful and energetic at school, which can deepen the downward spiral. We must make time for friends and family, not just to enhance our own health, but also to maintain the good health needed to be great teachers.

Our Students

Most important, we should care about our emotional health because of its effect on our students. This impact has become strikingly clear as I have watched my own children head off to school. Their moods and attitudes about school are largely shaped by their teachers' energy and attitudes. When their teachers are relaxed, happy, and healthy, Ethan and Carly bound onto the bus each morning. When they have had teachers who are constantly stressed out or disconnected emotionally from their students, they are more anxious and less enthusiastic about school.

Stressed-out and unhappy teachers mean stressed-out and unhappy children. What does a flight attendant explain when you are on the plane getting the safety prep before take-off? If there is a loss of cabin pressure, oxygen masks will fall from above. You must first put on your own mask before you try to help someone else. If we try to put others' needs before our own, not only will we not make it, but neither will the ones we are trying to help. Quite simply, you cannot give what you do not have. If we are to be healthy role models for our students and create happy, energetic, and safe learning environments, we must take good care of ourselves.

CHAPTER 2

Meeting Our Most Basic Needs

The educational community has seen a huge push over the past few years to make sure that students become more physically healthy. For example, the December 2009/January 2010 issue of *Educational Leadership* was titled "Health and Learning" and offered ideas for how to help students eat better, get more physically active, reconnect with nature, sleep well, and lower anxiety, in addition to several other topics. Negative reactions to the elimination of recess and concerns over the obesity crisis in young people in our country have peppered the news. Articles abound in educational newsletters advising us to get our students active and make sure they're eating healthy food. Many schools have begun tackling the problem of junk food in schools by prohibiting soda and candy for sale at lunch and in vending machines and by encouraging parents in elementary schools to provide healthy birthday treats in lieu of the traditional cupcakes. As teachers, we are becoming more and more conscious of the importance of helping our students develop healthy habits. In addition to wanting to teach children lifelong habits of self-care, we know that healthier kids will be more awake, have more energy for learning, and be more positively engaged academically and socially.

However, in a classic case of "Do as I say, not as I do," as teachers we don't take great care of our own basic needs as well as we should. (I remember once hiding the wrappers from my McDonald's bacon, egg, and cheese biscuits at the bottom of our class trash can in the middle of teaching a nutrition unit to my 5th graders.) We skip breakfast and load up on caffeinated coffee to get to school early enough to finish our planning. We scarf down starchy foods from the school cafeteria while rushing to make a couple of phone calls or run some copies during an already-too-short lunch break. We intentionally dehydrate ourselves because we have a three-hour stretch each morning when we don't have time to get to the bathroom. We stay up late grading papers, depriving ourselves of the vital sleep we need to attack each day with fresh energy. Exercise gets put off as we struggle to complete lesson plans and attend meetings. ("I'll run tomorrow," we promise ourselves.) We spend hours each weekend checking school e-mail, helping needy students, and communicating with parents, and we don't give ourselves time to strengthen our spirit. In short, we tend to neglect our own needs as we try to meet the needs of others.

And where does this pattern lead us? Fatigue builds as we couple a poor night's sleep with dehydration. By lunchtime, we are running on fumes since we haven't eaten an adequate breakfast. Because we haven't exercised in weeks, our energy is low anyway, and since we're eating a slice of greasy pizza and a couple of orange slices for lunch ("At least the orange slices are healthy," we reassure ourselves), our chances of getting a monster headache by 2:00 are pretty good.

Do any of these common teacher complaints sound familiar?

• "I'd love to exercise, and I know I'd feel better if I did, but when would I have time for that? I've got too much to do between taking care of my students *and* taking care of my family!"

• "I know I should eat better than I do, but I'm too busy getting lessons ready to worry about lunch until it's too late."

• "I get really cranky when I don't get enough sleep, but no one else is going to handle all of this student work for me."

If we were the only ones who suffered from this kind of deprivation, it would be one thing. But like the smoker who affects others in the room with second-hand smoke, our poor self-care has profound negative repercussions for our students. Because all we had was a doughnut and a cup of coffee for breakfast, our minds drift during a morning writing conference as our blood sugar drops. Because we didn't get enough sleep the night before, we snap impatiently at a student who didn't bring in his homework before we find out that his dog was just put to sleep. Once the buses leave, a colleague wants to do some planning together for an upcoming unit, and our lower-back pain and low energy lead us to avoid valuable collaboration. That night, we lug home our laptop and a pile of work, ready to exhaust ourselves yet again with another late night. ("I'll catch up on sleep this weekend," we lie to ourselves.)

So, are we doomed to poor physical and emotional health? No! Though there are certainly many challenges we face as teachers in this arena, there are also some ways we can take more control of our own well-being. Let's take a look at some of our most basic needs and examine why they may be challenging for us to meet. Then, and more importantly, let's see how we can better meet these needs within the context of a regular day of teaching.

Food: We Are What We Eat

What could be more basic to our health than the food we eat? You don't need me to tell you the importance of a good, balanced diet, right? However, getting that healthy diet can be tough when we teach. Especially if you are not a morning person, breakfast can be too easy to skip. Staff rooms seem to magnetically attract pastry trays and birthday cakes. Vending machines tempt even the healthiest and hardiest teacher when the afternoon munchies hit. And who can turn down a cute 2nd grader who appears at your door with a birthday cupcake?

Fortunately, we can leverage some elements of teaching to our advantage when it comes to healthy eating. For one thing, our schedules are so tight that we rarely have time to go out for lunch, so if we can just pack some healthier foods, we'll be pretty much stuck with them. Many of us have access to a refrigerator, either a shared one in a staff room or cafeteria or a small one in our own classroom, so we have a convenient place to keep healthy food if we bring it in. Also, most of us have a consistent schedule for when we eat lunch which can help us get into a healthy rhythm. So, let's break things down and see how we can take care of ourselves at various times of the day.

Breakfast

In researching this book, I have talked with countless teachers who told me they routinely skip breakfast on school days. They feel they simply aren't ready to eat so early before they're heading off to school or don't have the time. Others of us are unhealthy in different ways with breakfast. I remember during my first couple of years of teaching, I got into the habit of stopping at Dunkin' Donuts *and* McDonald's on my way to school in the morning. I'd get a large tea (with cream and sugar) at Dunkin' Donuts and then two (yes, count 'em, two) bacon, egg, and cheese biscuits and two (yes, that would be two again) hash browns. Gracious, it tasted good, but that regimen coupled with no exercise helped me gain over 20 pounds within two years.

Instead of skipping breakfast altogether or gorging ourselves on junk food, we have some pretty good alternatives if we have a hard time eating a healthy breakfast at home. Consider the following possibilities that you could keep at school:

• **Fruit and peanut butter.** Both can be kept at room temperature, which is a plus. Simply add a dab of peanut butter to each bite of banana or apple. This combo tastes great and has some protein to help get through a long morning.

• **Yogurt and granola.** Mix some granola cereal in with plain low- or nonfat yogurt, and you have a protein-rich meal to tide you over until lunch.

• **Cottage cheese.** I know, not everyone likes cottage cheese, but have you tried the flavored kind? The pineapple is my personal favorite, but there are other flavors, in convenient individual-size cups. A carton is more than enough to get you through a few hours.

• **Fruit and yogurt.** This one takes a little preparation, but it's tasty enough to be worth it. Slice an apple, pear, peach, banana, or whatever other fruit you like and mix it with some vanilla yogurt. You could also add some nuts or raisins.

• **Hard-boiled eggs.** You can prepare a bunch of these at once and keep them in the fridge. Again, the importance of protein in the morning can't be overstated!

Looking for more ideas? Try an Internet search of "healthy breakfast ideas" for a multitude of sites that might help.

Lunch

Although lunch may have a designated place in our schedules, it is often almost as neglected as breakfast for most teachers. Sure, our contracts guarantee us a duty-free lunch, but few teachers I know take that seriously. (We do when it comes time to negotiate our contracts, but few of us actually take a duty-free lunch. I guess it's important for us to know that we *could* even if we almost never do.) Instead of sitting down and eating a healthy lunch at a relaxed pace, we tend to eat bites of our sandwich while going through homework assignments. Or we eat quickly so we can make a couple of phone calls. Many times, I found myself so busy finalizing lesson plans for the afternoon that I often missed my lunch period entirely. Doing so meant that later in the day, I was nibbling away at my lunch as best I could between writing conferences or during transition times.

I encourage you to make a time to sit and really eat and relax. Even if you carve out just 10 minutes to read a magazine while you eat alone in your classroom or sit with a few colleagues in the staff room, giving yourself some downtime in the middle of the day will allow you to chew your food properly. You'll be less likely to have a stomachache later if you take some healthy time for lunch.

What about the food itself? Well, clearly, the healthier the food, the greater our energy will be for the remainder of the day. Of course, the challenge often is finding time to prepare a good lunch. It can be just too easy to eat a couple of cheeseburgers in the school cafeteria if we haven't brought something more nutritious for ourselves. Here are a few ideas for effective and quick ways to get some healthy meals for lunch:

• **Prepare extra dinner.** Whenever you're making dinner, prepare enough for at least one extra serving. As you clean up after dinner, pack the extra serving for the next day so it's waiting for you in the morning.

• **Check out ready-made lunches.** The environmentalist in me cringes at the packaging involved, but some good ready-made meals are available. Buy five and stick them in the fridge at school, and you're good for the week.

• **How's the cafeteria food?** As many schools begin to address the childhood obesity issue, salad bars and healthier lunch options are becoming more available in school cafeterias. If your school doesn't provide healthy alternatives, gather a group of like-minded colleagues together to address the problem. It will be good for you and your students!

Snacks

Admit it. You have candy stashed somewhere in your classroom. If you don't, you've got a neighbor who does, right? I know, I know. The rationalization is common: "I just can't make it through the afternoon without a little bit of chocolate!" One teacher I know (in a school where kids aren't allowed to bring in candy) actually has her chocolate tucked away in a lighthouse. Every time someone opens the lid for a piece, a foghorn sounds throughout the room.

The problem with snacks is that if they're around, they get eaten. There's a simple solution: bring only healthy snacks to school. If there's candy in the desk, it's awfully hard to turn it down at 3:15 when you're tired and your willpower is waning. (I may sound a bit smug about chocolate, but if I bring a can of Pringles into my room, they'll be gone by lunchtime.) If all you have around is an apple, that's going to taste pretty good when the 3:15 munchies hit.

Here are some snacks that are quick to prepare, easy to store, and healthy as well. As an added bonus, you'll be modeling healthy snacking for your students, and you can give them some ideas of good snacks that they can enjoy themselves.

• **Fresh fruit.** Buy a bag of apples or a bunch of bananas, and they'll be good for the week on a back shelf.

• **Dried fruit.** Dried apricots, dried apples, banana chips, raisins, and the like, can provide a nice shot of sugar in lieu of chocolate or other candy.

• **Cut-up veggies and salad dressing.** Sunday night, take 10 minutes to cut up carrots, broccoli, cucumbers, and other favorites, and create five containers with a mix of each. Keep a bottle of low-fat salad dressing at school, and you've got an easy dip for the veggies all week.

• **Trail mix.** Mixed nuts and raisins have fantastic staying power. There's a reason hikers rely on this snack to get through a long day on the trail. Just skip the M&Ms!

• **Cheese and crackers.** Don't go for the packaged stuff, which usually combines processed "fake" cheese and high-fat crackers. Cut up some cheese and keep a box of multigrain crackers on hand.

One teacher I work with shared an important tip: Know thyself! She learned that French fries were her weakness, so she had to come up with a suitable replacement for that craving. Microwave popcorn became her healthier substitute. Consider finding substitutes for the snack foods that get you in trouble. If you love candy, bring in a small piece of dark chocolate each day to replace the habit of a full Snickers bar. If sugary soda is your weak spot, sip cans of flavored seltzer. Try substituting potato chips with healthier crackers or pretzels.

What About the Stuff the Kids Bring In?

It's Valentine's Day, and seven of your kindergartners bring in boxes of chocolate for you. Your high school swim team is selling chocolate bars to raise money for new lane lines for the pool. Your middle school band is holding a bake sale for an upcoming trip. Fourth grade Girl Scouts arrive at your door with order forms (and you have a particular fondness for Thin Mints). We are bombarded with opportunities to support worthwhile student projects and causes throughout the year, and it seems as though most of these opportunities involve buying—and therefore eating—junk food. I once heard of an elementary school that hosted a "Donuts with Dad" (or what I like to call "Get Fat with Dad") promotion to get fathers into the school more. Once a week, kids could enjoy some Krispy Kremes before school with their dad for breakfast. Teachers were invited, too, of course!

So what do we do? We want to support important causes in our schools, and we certainly don't want to offend well-meaning parents and children. However, we know that if we bring home a box of cookies, we'll eat them. Here are a few ideas that might help navigate these tricky waters.

• **Donate without buying.** Instead of ordering the candy bars or buying the brownies, ask if you can make a donation without buying the product. You'll still be supporting the cause, but you won't have to fight with yourself later as you try not to eat the candy bar calling to you from your desk drawer.

• **Accept the treat and put it aside.** When 2nd grader Billy arrives at your door with a cupcake for his birthday, thank him profusely and tell him you'll save the cupcake for later. When no one's looking, throw it in the trash and enjoy the glow of self-righteous, strong willpower.

• **Don't "donate" it to the staff room.** Whatever you do, don't add to the junk food collection in your staff room by adding the box of Girl Scout cookies you're trying not to eat. You may be sabotaging someone else, and you know the cookies are there, so it's still tempting to snag a few later on!

Consider Keeping a Food Log

One year I was teaching a unit on nutrition with my 3rd graders. I had just watched the movie *Super Size Me*, and I was determined to work at teaching my students some healthier habits. For two weeks, my students all kept food logs, and I kept one right along with them. We recorded everything we ate and drank, both in school and at home, and we did some fun activities in conjunction with our journals. We practiced reading food labels and looked at how much sugar we ate on a daily basis. (Did you know that 4 grams of sugar is a teaspoon? That means that a can of Coke has about 12 teaspoons of sugar!) The food log ended up being a real revelation for me. For one thing, I hadn't realized before just how much I snacked. When I saw it all written down each day, I was appalled. I also found myself more conscious of what I was eating, simply because I knew I would have to write it down later. I encourage you to try this strategy as well. It's pretty interesting.

Beware of Using School as the Excuse

A good friend of mine who's a high school teacher was talking with me about his struggles with eating well during the school year. "I can be self-abusive with food," he admitted. "I've had two big spikes in my weight in the last few years. The first was when I first started teaching. The second was when I started teaching some online courses as a second job. It's almost like I need to punish myself for working too much. I know it doesn't make sense." He said that he got into the routine of using school as the excuse for poor eating habits. For example, he would order a pizza for dinner, telling himself, "I'm just too tired to cook, and I have too much work to do," when deep down, he knew that fixing a sandwich or some other quick and healthy dinner wouldn't have taken any more time or energy than ordering and picking up the pizza. Our overwhelming workloads and hectic schedules can be just the excuse we're looking for to get into unhealthy eating patterns.

Another teacher I talked to suggested that some people use their hard work or a hard day as a justification for eating poorly. "I've had a tough day. I deserve a bowl of ice cream before bed!" Instead, let's use those same factors to nudge ourselves into healthy patterns. It's a mind-set shift, but one that we can do. Instead of insisting that a bad day warrants a bowl of ice cream, we might tell ourselves, "I've had a tough day; I deserve to be healthy." Another shift might be instead of saying, "I just don't have time to get some healthy food. My students' needs have to come first," we can just as simply say, "I can't afford to be low on energy. My students need me at my best."

Hydration: The Teacher's Lament, or "I Don't Even Have Time to Pee!"

As I spoke with teachers all over the country in various settings, one of the most common daily struggles they described was finding time to go to the bathroom. High school and middle school teachers often have to contend with back-to-back 90- minute blocks of teaching time. Many elementary school teachers have three hours or more when they are in charge of their classes. Some teachers also have to contend with bathrooms that are far away from their classrooms, making it almost impossible for them to step away for a quick bathroom break. Many teachers today feel, or have been told, that for safety and liability reasons, they can't leave students unattended even for a minute. So, instead of sipping water throughout the day as we know we should, we intentionally dehydrate ourselves. Drinking enough water is one of the most basic things we can do to keep ourselves healthy. Good hydration can help cut the risk of disease, enhance mental clarity, improve digestion, relieve back and joint pain, and help control body weight, among other things (Rodgers, 2007). Ensuring that we stay properly hydrated should be a basic goal as we map out how to take great care of ourselves. Waiting too long to go to the bathroom can help cause urinary tract and bladder infections (Cornforth, 2009), so it's not surprising that several teachers also mentioned that their doctors have said teachers seem to suffer from these problems more than other people. Here are a few ways to be proactive about this issue so that we can drink the water we need to:

- **Use a neighbor.** Make a pact with a nearby teacher: "You watch my class, and I'll watch yours." Plan the times of day that are easiest for you to have your colleague cover your class for a few minutes.
- **Use support staff.** I had a special education teacher who came to my room every day at the same time to have reading conferences with some struggling readers. Because she was a certified teacher, I could leave the class for a couple of minutes when she was there.
- **Ask for administrative help.** Let your principal know if your schedule is unreasonable. Work toward creating humane schedules for adults in your building.

In some schools, the problem is different. You may not have easy access to clean, cold water. Perhaps the water fountain is way down the hall, or it may be that you're nervous about drinking city water. We may even justify our addiction to diet cola with these sorts of explanations, knowing full well that water would be healthier. Consider bringing in your own water to sip throughout the day. Put a half-full bottle in the freezer the night before and fill the rest of the bottle in the morning. You'll be surprised at how long the water will stay cold.

Exercise

How many of us struggle with getting into a good exercise routine? As with poor eating habits, our crazy school schedules can be just the excuse we're looking for to put off exercising. "I'm just too tired to run," or "I've got too many meetings after school," or any number of other such laments are common. And yet, we also know the benefits of good exercise. We have more energy, are in a better mood, are less affected by stress, and feel better about ourselves when we exercise consistently (and these pluses are in addition to the myriad of other health benefits). Not only is it possible, but it's vital that we build time into our schedule for exercise. We will be better teachers when we do. When figuring out how to make exercise part of your day, consider the following points:

• **Twenty minutes is enough.** Don't feel like you have to go to the gym for an hour for your workout to be worthwhile. Go for a brisk walk every day for 20 minutes, and you'll benefit. Even breaking that 20 minutes into 10- or even 5-minute blocks throughout the day is beneficial.

• **Make the time consistent and nonnegotiable.** It's easy to skip a day here and there. "I've got a meeting after school, so I'll just skip this once" is an invitation to skip again, and again, and again. Once you've established a routine of exercising, you won't have to battle yourself to get going—it will become as automatic as brushing your teeth before you go to bed.

• **Make exercise part of your work routine.** Here's another opportunity to leverage our strict school schedules to our advantage. If exercise is part of your work schedule, it's easy to stick with it. I used to swim from 5:30 a.m. to 6:30 a.m., take a shower, and head right in to school. I rarely missed a day, because swimming was part of my morning routine to get to school. If afternoons work better for you, consider making exercise part of how you get home.

• **Exercise with a group.** A group of teachers at a school I used to work at went for a power walk through the neighborhood every day after dismissal. I have a group I swim with in the mornings. Knowing that others will be with you can be incredibly motivational.

• **Do an activity you find pleasurable.** I have a hard time sticking with running. Unless I'm with someone else, I quit early and skip often. I just don't love to run. Swimming, in contrast, is fun for me. I love the feel of water rushing over my body. I find it enjoyable to push myself through a tough set. The value of the exercise itself being enjoyable can't be overstated. Whether it's biking, running, hiking, spinning, yoga, walking, kayaking, or any other activity, if you enjoy doing it, it will be much easier to stick to your routine. You might even combine something you enjoy with a form of exercise to make it more fun. For example, set up an exercise bike in front of the TV to watch your favorite shows while you work out. Download some fun podcasts to take with you as you walk or run. Whatever you can do to make exercise more enjoyable, do it.

• **Exercise with students.** A 4th grade teacher I worked with in Connecticut started a running club for upper-grade students at our school. Three days a week, she headed out to the track with about 20 kids to run, walk, and talk. If students are counting on you to be there, it's awfully hard not to show up. As a bonus, you'll be teaching and modeling healthy exercise habits for your students.

• **Move while you work.** Some teachers told me that they made a point of moving a lot as they worked. One high school teacher said that he creates learning activities that involve student movement (e.g., having kids stand and circulate as they share ideas), because he moves when they do. A middle school teacher told me that she got rid of her desk so that she would have to move to her students when they needed help, instead of them coming to her. Get a pedometer to record how many steps you take in a day. Take brisk walks to the office a couple of times a day. Park your car farther away from the entrance to your school. If your school has an elevator, take the stairs. Instead of sitting in a chair, bend your knees and squat, or create a standing workstation. There are any number of small changes we can make to get our bodies moving a little more as we work.

Record Your Progress

It can be surprisingly motivating to record the exercise you do each day. Make the process quick and easy so it doesn't turn into just one more thing to do. Create a simple chart, either on your computer or in a notebook that gives you a way to record the kind and amount of exercise you do each day (see Figure 2.1 for an example). I recommend keeping this log at school, to emphasize in your own mind that staying healthy is an essential part of your job.

Sleep

Sleep is another fundamental need. The scientific research on what happens when people don't get enough sleep is well documented. Sleep loss impairs memory and cognitive functioning, decreases performance and alertness, and increases people's risks for injury and illness (Breus, 2006). The fact that sleep

Figure 2.1	Exercise Log	
Date	**Type of Exercise**	**Amount**
5.10.10	Walking	20 min. (1.5 miles)
5.11.10	Walking	20 min. (1.5 miles)
	Gardening	1 hour
5.13.10	Biking…easy…around town	1 hour (about 10 miles)
5.14.10	Walking	30 min. (2 miles)
	Sit-ups	25
5.15.10	Walking	30 min. (15 min. before school and 15 min. after)

deprivation has been used as a form of torture is another clue to the importance of getting good sleep.

However, good sleep can be hard to come by for teachers. We often stay up too late correcting assignments or planning the next day's lessons. A tough interaction with a colleague or a parent plays over and over in our minds as we stare at the ceiling in the middle of the night.

Here's a time when our strict schedules can again work in our favor. How much sleep do you need to feel rested? What time do you need to be up each morning? Once you've got those two questions answered, give yourself a bedtime and stick to it. If you need eight hours of sleep and must be up at 5:30 to be ready for school on time, force yourself to stick to a 9:30 bedtime. Make sure to disconnect from school with a good book, some meditation, a hot shower, or any other strategy that will get your brain ready to rest. You'll have more energy, and your students will benefit as a result.

Physical Safety

Though schools are generally safe environments—or at least should be— many teachers must deal with issues of personal safety every day at work. Here are just a few of the stories I heard as I talked with teachers:

• One teacher in an upscale Northeast district had to wear a walkie-talkie at all times, lock her classroom door when students were in class, and memorize code words to give to the office. These precautions were necessary because one of her 2nd graders was the son of semiroyalty in Europe and was a likely kidnapping target.

• A high school teacher in rural Maine was threatened to be stabbed by a student who was already on parole.

• Teachers in Chicago spoke of walking in pairs or small groups to their cars each afternoon because of gang violence in the neighborhood. They also avoid staying at school after dusk.

It can be awfully hard to focus on teaching our students when we're worried about staying safe. Here are a few ideas to consider if you find yourself in such a situation:

• **Talk with administration.** Make sure your administrators know about any kind of dangerous situation. Ask specific questions about what you should do and how they will support you.

• **Get help from colleagues.** Ask other teachers for advice and help. It might be as simple as asking someone to walk with you to your car each day. You might just need someone to listen to a struggle you're having. You might even need to call in a union representative for some cases.

• **Know when to get out.** After the previously mentioned high school teacher was threatened to be stabbed by one of his students, and he realized his administration wasn't going to support him, he left the school. It was probably the right thing to do. In extreme cases like this, you may need to make a tough decision about whether you feel safe enough at your school to stay there.

Physical Conditions of Our Schools

Another basic element of staying physically (and therefore emotionally) healthy is having a healthy environment in which to teach. The basic cleanliness and physical appearance of our schools and classrooms can have a profound effect on the way we feel at work. Our surroundings can help us relax and focus on the work at hand, or they can add to our stress levels and make us cranky and irritable.

Although the average teacher who has been around for a while has been exposed to so many germs that he or she could probably be dipped in a vat of Ebola virus with few discernible ill effects, we should still focus on keeping our classrooms as clean and germ-free as possible. When cold and flu season hit, invest in a bottle of hand sanitizer, and require your students to use a little on their way into class. Take a couple of minutes to spray down desks and tables at the end of the day. That five minutes a day could save you a week of sick days later in the year.

In addition to being clean germ-wise, a classroom should also be neat and tidy in appearance. Having to work day in and day out in a cluttered and disorganized room is bad for the nerves of students and teachers alike. I remember one room that was especially challenging when I moved into it. Duct tape held sections of the carpet together. The walls were painted the baby blue that I strongly associate with gas station bathrooms. Dark brown wood paneling (it was actually thick cardboard of some kind) graced one wall underneath two enormous chalkboards. I knew if I was going to be happy in this classroom, I needed to invest a little time and energy in some improvements. Here are some ideas for addressing these kinds of physical challenges in our classrooms:

• **Cover things up.** If you can't stand chalkboards (the dust drives me crazy!), cover them with corkboard or colored paper. They are great display spaces if you don't need to write on them. Area rugs can cover up missing floor tiles (or duct tape on the carpeting). A well-placed print or poster can hide a hole in a wall.

• **Paint a wall.** The color of a classroom has a huge impact on the tone of the work environment. Bright yellow, orange, and red can raise anxiety levels and increase aggression. Dull and pasty light blues and cream colors look bland and boring and can put people to sleep. Instead look for warm yellows and browns and earthy greens and blues. Try painting one wall a bold color and another wall white to make your room look and feel bigger. Consider going to a hardware store and asking salespeople there about their paint rejects. Most stores have gallons of paint for sale that have been returned by other customers. I picked up a $5 can of woodsy green for one wall of the classroom described earlier, and it totally changed the look of the room.

- **Bring in homey touches.** A nice floor lamp, some tropical plants, and a couple of simple and comfy canvas chairs can make a classroom space feel more inviting and warm.
- **Eliminate unused or unneeded furniture.** I once visited a cramped 2nd grade classroom that had 37 places to sit for only 18 children! Consider removing furniture that doesn't get used. (Do you really sit at your teacher's desk?) An open and uncluttered classroom feels relaxed and comfortable. For more great classroom design ideas, check out *Classroom Spaces That Work* by Marlynn Clayton and Mary Beth Forton (2001).

Take Care of Your Spirit

We've all had those days where we leave school feeling defeated and disheartened. A student who had been making great progress has a rough day and screams, "I hate you!" as she storms out of the room. The superintendent releases the latest round of standardized tests results and admonishes the staff for not working hard enough to bring up the scores. We hear through the gossip grapevine at school that a colleague is upset with us for something we said at last week's staff meeting. These and other kinds of moments can leave us not just physically exhausted, but emotionally drained. It's hard to get up the next day and have good energy for our students with these episodes leaving a sour taste in our mouths. Having a few strategies for recharging our inner selves can allow us to shake off the tough interactions that are a part of the important work we do.

Find Ways to Disconnect From School

It's important for us to disconnect when work is done. I found this much easier to do when I became a dad. There's nothing like stacking cups with a one-year-old for shaking off a discouraging staff meeting! When my children, Ethan and Carly, were really little, my wife, Heather, who stayed at home full time, needed some down time when I got home. She would retreat to the kitchen to sip wine, watch mindless TV, and *slowly* prepare dinner. My job was to play with (or deal with, depending on the day) the kids. By the time dinner was over, many of the smaller worrisome events from the day had simply melted away. Spending time with family is just one of a variety of ways we can disconnect from a long hard day.

My wife says that knitting is a way she can get out of her own head. I know just what she means. Knitting is an engaging activity for her that requires a degree of concentration while being a bit mindless at the same time. Jigsaw and Sudoku puzzles do the same thing for me. There are any number of ways we can "get out of our heads" when we need to disconnect such as exercising, cooking, listening to an audio book, playing the piano, or reading a fun book. The list is endless. Find a couple of these kinds of activities and haul them out after a tough day.

Engage in Personal Reflection and Spiritual Growth

There are many ways we can reflect on what is going well in our lives and think about how we can change for the better. Whether we're going through a rough stretch or not, finding ways to reflect and grow as a person can help keep us grounded and sane. The following suggestions offer some ways to keep our spirits strong.

• **Read your favorite book.** Whenever I'm going through a rough stretch, I pull out one of my favorite books, *The Screwtape Letters* by C. S. Lewis. This series of letters from an experienced devil to his apprentice nephew who is learning to tempt the soul of a man always gives me something new to think about. I find it comforting and thought-provoking at the same time. Is there a particular book that soothes your spirit or helps you reflect? Consider pulling it off the shelf and rereading it every now and then.

• **Practice meditation and prayer.** Setting aside time for quiet contemplation can give us the space required to think deeply. Whether it's five minutes every night before bed or a couple of longer times during the week, the key is to create a consistent routine for quiet reflection and stick to it.

• **Journal.** Like meditation and prayer, journaling can be a great way to deeply process things that are going on in our lives. Taking a few minutes each day to think and record our thoughts through writing can lead us to answer questions, raise new questions, and come to insights that might not have occurred otherwise. Journaling also provides a record of our thinking and growth over time that can allow us to look back and reflect even more deeply.

• **Talk with a counselor or confidant.** In my mid-20s, whenever I needed to discuss a personal challenge or problem, I would find myself driving from Connecticut to Virginia for a weekend trip to visit my grandmother. A former counselor for clergy members in Southern Maine for many years, she was my unofficial spiritual guide. My grandmother's objectivity and different perspectives often helped me process and think through complicated issues. Having a confidant, whether he or she is a professional counselor, a religious leader, a close friend, or a family member, can be a great asset in refreshing and deepening our spirits.

• **Participate in an organized religion.** Finding a community of people who engage in spiritual growth together can be very powerful. When people come together as a part of a church, synagogue, mosque, or other religious sanctuary, they are able to engage in spiritual growth with others who are asking similar questions and looking for guidance and growth.

There's nothing like engaging in spiritual enrichment to help gain some much needed perspective in our lives. Contemplating the grandness and mystery of the greater good and powers beyond ourselves can help renew our sense of purpose in life and let go of some of life's daily struggles. Organized religion, meditation, reading spiritually enriching writings, and communing with nature are just a few ways we can work at enlarging our spirit and reflecting on life in new and powerful ways.

Connect with Nature

One of the ways that we can refresh our spirit and grow spiritually is through a connection with nature, and I believe that this is a vastly underappreciated challenge of our profession. Most of us spend our days surrounded by concrete, tile, metal, and plastic. Many teachers (especially in urban settings) have window views that show parking lots or other buildings. Some teachers don't even have windows. When I taught in the Northeast, I often had winter days where I got to school before the sun came up and didn't leave the building until it was already dark. Richard Louv, in his book *Last Child in the Woods: Saving our Children from Nature-Deficit Disorder* (2005), makes the compelling case for why it's so important for children to stay connected with nature. I believe the same is true for adults. There's nothing like a hike on a nature trail, a walk at the beach, or pulling some weeds out of the garden for washing our inner selves clean of all of the frustrations and negative energy that accumulate daily.

Connect with Nature at School

Some teachers are lucky enough to have easy access to nature at their schools. I've visited schools that have nature paths incorporated right onto the school grounds. One school I saw in Northern Virginia actually had signs posted throughout the trail. ("A pile of rocks is a great way to attract small animals. Look for lizards, snakes, toads, and mice!") How cool is that? I've seen other schools that are surrounded by fields and woods that make it easy to take a stroll and unwind during a lunch break.

There are many ways we can bring elements of nature right into our classrooms. These ideas are especially helpful if you teach in an urban setting and you aren't able to just walk outside into the woods.

• **Bring some house plants into your classroom.** Get a couple of cheap low-light plants to place in your classroom. Watering and pulling off a few dead leaves can be your little nature break during the day. As a bonus, your classroom space will have a more pleasant feel that is conducive for good learning.

• **Bring in a fish tank or class pet.** The sound of water running in an aquarium can provide a pleasant background sound throughout the day, and watching the fish can be a great way to relax. If an aquarium is too much work, consider a small pet that is easy to take care of and doesn't require much work, such as a hermit crab or small lizard. One year, my neighboring teacher set up a small terrarium in her room and invited her 5th graders to bring in toads, bugs, and worms. They had a working terrarium all year that was really fun!

• **Bring in a water fountain.** Look for a desktop water fountain and place it near your work space. The sight and sound of running water can be quite soothing.

• **Feed the birds.** If you have a window in your classroom, get a small window bird feeder to attract birds to your window!

Connect Nature to Your Curriculum

Nature journaling can be a great inspiration for poetry. A music teacher can have students observe the sounds outside and recreate them using musical instruments. Local nature centers can provide incredible support for your science curriculum and make for fantastic field trips. I once saw a vertical team of K-5 teachers do an integrated science, math, reading, and writing unit through gardening. Mixed-graded groups of students created a vegetable garden together in the spring, took care of it through the summer, and had a feast in the fall! With a little creativity and imagination, you may also be able to figure out how to get outside a little more with your students.

Connect to Nature Outside of School

Find a place you that you can go to get recharged after a tough day. It could be as simple as a park bench near a river in town. After a tough day or week, take a book and just go sit. If you have a family, take a family hike. It will be good for all of you!

You might also consider creating an outside work space for yourself for the inevitable after-school work that we bring home. You might actually look forward to correcting those science tests if there was a picnic table near a bird feeder!

Conclusion

There's no doubt that it can be hard to take care of ourselves really well, and given the number of topics explored and ideas given in this chapter, it might feel overwhelming to know where to start. Perhaps several areas in our lives could use improvement at any given time. My suggestion is to choose only one for now and make a plan. Perhaps you'll try keeping a food log for the next two weeks and see what comes up. Maybe you'll carve out 20 minutes after school each day to take a walk. Getting some plants into your classroom could be a good place to start. Whatever you choose, try something and see how it goes.

Remember, we're not being selfish when we take care of ourselves! *Au contraire!* When we make sure that we take care of our most basic needs, we will be in much better shape to be effective caregivers for others. No one else is going to do these things for us, so we'd better take care of them ourselves. Our students deserve no less.

SPOTLIGHT ON A HEALTHY TEACHER

Sherry,* 3rd Grade Teacher

Sherry had always struggled with keeping a healthy weight. "When I was a kid," she explained, "food was the way our family provided comfort. If you had a bad day, Mom took you out for ice cream. If you were sad, you had a piece of candy. Every family gathering was about food."

Being a teacher did not help. Although she fixed herself healthy foods at school, she rarely ate breakfast because of her hectic morning routine, so in the evening, she tended to overeat. She also kept a jar of candy hidden away in her classroom closet, so in the afternoons when she was tired and her willpower was low, she tended to pick away at the candy jar, a piece here and a piece there.

At age 55, Sherry had a scare. Her doctor told her point-blank, "You are showing signs of developing type 2 diabetes, and you are developing bone spurs in your heels from carrying excess weight."

Sherry went to a dietitian who asked her to keep a food log for two weeks and recommended some changes. The most surprising one was that she had to eat *more*. "I was trying to diet by starving myself of protein," said Sherry. "I had to learn to eat more protein, more fruits and vegetables, and cut out the candy and chips. It actually wasn't that hard. I started precutting apples and celery to bring to school. I gave myself more time in the morning to eat breakfast, and I made sure to eat some protein to jump-start my energy and metabolism."

Sherry also started to exercise. She was already an avid gardener, but she became more conscious of doing knee bends and squats while planting and weeding. She also started to walk. Every day after school, she walked briskly around the neighborhood for about 30 minutes.

At a recent weigh-in with her dietitian, Sherry found that she had lost a total of 80 pounds. She reports that her energy level and her mood at school have both greatly improved. "I have more patience with students and colleagues," she admits. "I feel better about myself and have more confidence."

*Sherry, like all of the teachers mentioned in these Spotlights throughout the book, is based on real teachers whom I interviewed.

CHAPTER 3

Belonging: Becoming an Important Part of a Community

People are social creatures. It's simply a human trait. Whether we are introverts or extroverts, shy or gregarious, we need to know that we are part of a community. We need to feel that we have others with whom we connect and who share commonalities. We need to feel accepted for who we are and to be known for our strengths. In his classic paper "A Theory of Human Motivation," psychologist Abraham Maslow (1943) placed the need for belonging just after basic physiological and safety needs in his hierarchy of human needs.

Just as with our most basic needs discussed in the previous chapter, we tend to be more conscious of helping our students meet this need than ourselves. Many schools set aside time at the beginning of the year to build community within classrooms and the greater school community. Pep rallies and yearbooks in high school, cohort teams in middle schools, and daily morning meetings in elementary schools all speak to our belief in and attention to helping students feel accepted and socially connected. Many colleges have first-year students come to campus a week before upperclassmen to bond and create social connections before classes begin for this same reason.

It is important to recognize that teachers have this same basic need for belonging as well, and just like our students, we will be happier and healthier (and therefore better teachers) if we have meaningful connections with other people.

Meeting this need outside of school is vitally important. Having solid friends and supportive family members, belonging to sports teams, participating in church groups, joining a book club and other social networks are just a few great ways to have a sense of belonging in our lives. After a tough day at school, these social connections can help us re-center ourselves and allow us to feel a sense of balance and strength.

It is just as vitally important that we feel a positive sense of belonging at school. Consider that during an average week, we spend about half of our waking hours at work. When we know that we feel connected with others and feel accepted at school, we are more positively engaged. This chapter will explore ways we can nurture productive and healthy relationships with various groups of people who we connect with at school—colleagues, administrators, students, families, and the wider educational community.

Building Relationships with Colleagues

When I first began teaching, I remember hearing teachers express sadness that being a classroom teacher was so isolating. "You go into your classroom at 9:00 and come out at 3:00, and you never get to see any other adults!" was the oft-heard refrain. This aspect of teaching has changed dramatically in many schools. Working with colleagues is now a daily occurrence for most of us. In one recent year, I had two full-time paraprofessionals in my classroom. I also worked at least once a week with a speech and language therapist, an occupational therapist, a physical therapist, two special education teachers, two school counselors, and two other paraprofessionals who supported students in my class. That's 11 different adults in addition to myself who regularly worked with students in my class! There were times when I found myself pining for the days when teaching *was* all about shutting your door and just working with kids.

In addition to the number of support staff that several teachers work with, our profession is becoming more collegial in other ways. Many of us now work on committees with other teachers to develop curricula or schoolwide initiatives. We may have mentoring and induction programs where teachers observe and support other teachers. In one school where I worked, we had periodic walk-throughs where teams of professionals visit every classroom to see how our literacy instruction was progressing throughout the entire school. We may use team teaching or collaborate with colleagues on particular units. There is no doubt in my mind that teachers work with colleagues more than ever before.

This collaboration can be both wonderful and challenging. On the one hand, our wish has been granted: we no longer have many days where we see few other adults. This contact provides opportunities to share ideas, learn from each other, and support each other with challenges and problems. A side benefit is that if our professional relationships are collegial, students get to see models for how people work together respectfully.

On the other hand, these increased interactions can also cause friction and discord. Mickey Corso, a consultant from the Quaglia Institute for Student Aspirations, once highlighted the challenges of all of this adult interaction at a staff meeting at our school. "We got into this profession because we're really good at working with children," he began. "But there's a shadow side to that …. We may be really good with children, but we're not so good with adults!" Our staff chuckled uncomfortably as we realized that he was on to something. Think of how nervous many of us get when an open house rolls around. And what is open house? We get up in front of a group of people and talk. It is what we do every day when we are teaching. So why do many teachers find it so nerve-wracking? An audience filled with adults is one we may find intimidating. This is just one small illustration of how teachers may struggle with heightened collaboration.

Seek Out Enthusiastic Colleagues

One of the best things we can do for ourselves that will help us boost our sense of belonging at school is to get connected with colleagues who have great energy and passion for teaching. This is especially important in a large school where it can be easy to get lost in a sea of teachers and support staff. I am not advocating starting a clique, but I am advocating finding a few trusted colleagues whom you can turn to when things are tough or who may be willing to take on some fun projects with you. Consider some of the following ideas as a jumping-off place for figuring out how to connect professionally with staff at your school:

• **Organize a regular reflection time.** This gathering might be a formal group that meets every Wednesday to discuss a particular topic, or it may be an informal walk-and-talk around the school grounds after school. Invite all staff, and keep the time consistent.

• **Explore education books together.** Put out a note to staff: "I'm reading *X book*, and I'd love to have some company! Join me this Tuesday at 7:30 a.m. if you're interested, and we'll set some discussion times."

• **Start a goal-specific group.** If you have a particular professional goal (e.g., getting better at writing conferences, integrating the arts into science, or aligning the new state standards with the reading curriculum), invite interested staff members to join in your efforts.

• **Ask for release time.** It can be hard for many staff to get to school early or to stay late. Ask an administrator how you and fellow staff members can get coverage from other responsibilities (e.g., cafeteria duty or other committee work) so that more people can participate.

• **Set up an observation rotation.** There's nothing like observing in a colleague's room. You learn so much by listening to another teacher and watching how he or she teaches. Set up a rotation for interested staff so that all can participate. Have an administrator help with coverage.

Make Friends with Professional Peers

"A staff who plays together stays together!" So said a teacher on why she felt her own staff was so tight. Another teacher from the same school told me, "Some of our staff members are hysterical! There are always a few teachers around here who can make you laugh." While it's important to connect with colleagues professionally, developing friendships and positive social groups at school can nurture your sense of belonging in other ways. When friends know who you are outside of school, they can lend important emotional support when things are tough. When a friend of ours was battling cancer recently, it meant a great deal to me that a couple of friends on staff kept checking in to see how we were doing. Friends can also add an element of fun to the school day that helps us have better energy throughout the day.

I recently visited an elementary school in Pennsylvania where teachers have developed incredibly strong friendships. It was evident by the way they joked and playfully teased each other throughout the day and by the positive energy they brought to their work together. These teachers even have a staff volleyball team and a whole display case in the front of the school devoted to pictures, news articles, and awards from the team. Just imagine the positive message this team sends to kids at this school! Not only are their teachers happier and healthier because of the bonds they have formed, but students also observe great role models for strong adult friendships.

Here are some other ideas that teachers have successfully used to foster friendships at school:

• **Invite staff to weekly breakfasts.** Meet at a local diner once a week for coffee and breakfast.

• **Go to happy hour together on Friday.** Send an e-mail to the staff: "Everyone's invited! Meet at Jimmy's Grill for some nachos at 4:00."

• **Join a staff sports team.** Indoor soccer, tennis, golf, running, volleyball, rowing—the possibilities are endless. Staff members who do not want to play can still participate by coming to cheer on the team.

• **Start a walking club.** Get a couple of people to commit (so you always have a few), and then invite everyone to join. Keep the days and times consistent so people can plan for it.

• **Begin a book club (for non-school-related books).** Teachers who may not want to join a club about educational books may be up for a good novel. Book clubs often bring together staff members with varied interests and personalities from many parts of the school.

• **Put on a staff talent show.** One high school teacher told me that when his staff put on a talent show, teachers from different departments formed new friendships that were not there before.

- **Be especially mindful to include new staff members.** Go out of your way to invite staff members who are new to your building. They may be nervous about joining an activity and could use some extra encouragement.
- **Watch a game together.** Invite everyone to meet at someone's house or at a local sports pub to cheer on the local favorite team (just not the Yankees, okay?). Or attend your students' sports meets together.

Dealing with a Toxic Environment

Also affecting our ability to build relationships with colleagues is the culture at school. Some schools have tight-knit staffs that not only work well together professionally but also go out for happy hour on Fridays and get together on the weekends. Other schools have toxic workplace environments with vicious gossiping, professional backstabbing, ugly social cliques, and open hostility. Roland Barth (2006), founding director of the Principals' Center at Harvard University, outlines four common types of relationships found in schools: parallel play, adversarial relationships, congeniality, and collegiality.

I have had the experience of working in one school that was truly collegial and another that was adversarial, and the difference in my physical and emotional energy between the two was unbelievable. In the first, I looked forward to seeing my colleagues each day and welcomed chances to work on committees. In the second, I avoided interactions as much as possible with all but a few trusted friends. This is not a book about how to change school cultures. Instead, this section will offer some strategies for how you as an individual teacher can nurture healthy collegial relationships, which, as a pleasant side effect, may have a positive impact on the overall culture of your school.

- **Do not become negative yourself.** Sometimes we can accidentally meet our need for belonging by being negative ourselves. People who groan and complain together can feel great comradery, but wallowing in pessimism will not do ourselves any real good in the long run and will inevitably transfer to our students.
- **Engage in crucial conversations.** According to best-selling author David Maxfield (2009), teachers who have crucial conversations with unsupportive

administrators and colleagues lower their levels of stress and are significantly more satisfied at school. All too often, we teachers shy away from difficult conversations, and this avoidance increases the chances we will burn out.

• **Find at least one positive colleague.** If you have at least one colleague with whom you can connect positively, you will feel a semblance of belonging on staff, which can make some of the other challenges with adversarial staff members more bearable.

• **Connect with the broader educational community.** Nurturing collegial relationships outside your own school can be a lifesaver. Check out the specific ideas at the end of this chapter.

• **Be realistic about how long you can stay on a school's faculty.** I once stayed too long. I kept telling myself, "It will get better next year." Take a brutally honest assessment of where your school is headed. If the culture is not changing, get out. Find a school that is a better match, and you will be a healthier, happier, and, yes, better teacher.

Building Relationships with Administrators

Having an administrator who is on our side can let us be more comfortable and relaxed as professionals. When we know our administrators well, and they know us, we can take sound professional risks and count on their support when we need it. The sense of belonging that comes from knowing that our administrators know us can help us feel safe and comfortable at school.

Be Proactive

We need to be proactive because, unfortunately, most administrators do not have time to be the true educational leaders that they wish they could be. Swamped by the administrivia of their positions, they struggle with finding the time to observe in our classrooms, coach our teaching, or build solid relationships with us. In 15 years as a public school teacher, I was officially observed by my principal a grand total of three times. Some years, an assistant principal took over. Some years, my principal was just too swamped, and knowing that kids and parents were happy, I think she figured she had bigger fish to fry. Although a certain amount of relief accompanies not having the dreaded "formal observation," I was professionally frustrated as well. How will my principal know me as a teacher if she never observes me in action? How will I get better as a teacher if I never get any coaching?

Fortunately, we can better connect with our administrators in many ways. Here are a few ideas:

• **Invite them in.** When your high school kids are putting the finishing touches on the final drafts of their essays, jot a quick note to your administrator and invite him in for five minutes. When your kindergartners are putting on a puppet show, send a quick e-mail letting your principal know when it is happening. Keep these invitations low-key and frequent, and your principal will be in your room more often.

• **Copy them on home-school communication.** Whenever you are sending home a note to parents, send a copy to your principal. He or she will have a better idea of what you're doing in your classroom and will feel in the loop, making it easier to stay connected with you.

• **Pop into the office.** Every now and then, stroll over to the principal's office and check in with a quick "How's it going?" Even though they are surrounded by people, administrators often feel isolated, and frequent check-ins from staff members are welcome opportunities to share their own successes and struggles.

Beware of Becoming Too Close

When we feel connected with administrators, we strengthen our sense of belonging in our schools. When we become close friends and confidants of our administrators, we risk losing our sense of belonging with our colleagues. Though it is natural for administrators to become friends with some staff members, those staff members may have to deal with the adult equivalent of wedgies and noogies that teachers' pets endure on the playground. Tread these waters cautiously, if at all!

Building Relationships with Students

For many teachers, creating and maintaining personal connections with students is as natural as breathing. The payoffs for students who are connected to their teachers are important. When students know that we know them, they are more connected with school, are more likely to persevere when challenged, and enjoy school more. I contend that the payoffs for teachers are just as great. When we are connected with our students, we are more engaged and energetic. School has more meaning and purpose when we are tied more to our students than to the content we teach.

Years ago, many teachers were advised not to connect personally with students, but few educational leaders still adhere to this outmoded idea. Most elementary schools have the model of self-contained classrooms so that students are with the same teacher all day. Middle schools generally team students together so that young adolescents have a consistent peer group and small team of teachers who all get to know one another well. Many high schools create advisory groups where teachers get to work with a small consistent group of students, so the students have a trusted adult who knows them well. But again, I contend that there is just as much in it for us.

Although I am strongly advocating becoming connected with our students, I advise against becoming friends with our students. When we are personally connected, teachers and students can share interests and have positive interactions. However, there still needs to be a hierarchical nature to the relationships. If we are counting on students to be an emotional support for us, we are in dangerous territory. We are ultimately here for our students, not the other way around.

Get to Know Your Students

A few years ago, I attended a workshop run by Don Graves, a longtime writer and advocate for teachers and children, and he had a great litmus test to see how well we know our students (see also Graves, 2006, pp. 3–4). Create a three-columned chart. In the left column, write the names of the students in your class, in the order in which you think of them. It is interesting, in and of itself, to see whom you think of first and whom you struggle to remember. In the second column, write down one thing that you know about each student that has nothing to do with school—for example, the number of siblings she has, where he spent last weekend, favorite sports, hobbies, and so forth. In the third column, write a check mark if you have talked with this student about this nonschool thing.

When we create and maintain authentic and meaningful relationships with students, they tend to be more connected with and invested in school. And here's the great part: so are we! The majority of our school day is spent with students, so it only makes sense to make sure we enjoy their company. Getting to know them and letting them know that they are important to us is a great way for us to feel a greater sense of belonging at school.

The point here is clear: not only is it important that we know our students, but they need to know that we know them! When they do, they will be more connected to us and school, they will be more engaged and willing to work, and we will all reap the rewards.

Here are some additional ways you can connect with your students:

• **Build in time for chitchat.** Invest a bit of time each day in class to having relaxed social conversations with students. Maybe it is the first five minutes as kids enter the room. Perhaps it is the last five minutes of the day. Keep this time consistent, relaxed, and make sure to talk with everyone each week. You might even keep a simple note sheet or checklist handy to make sure you are connecting with all students.

• **Eat in the cafeteria.** Good grief—not every day, but how about once a week? It is amazing how different many students are when they are eating lunch. You will get to know them much better.

• **Create a personal display space.** On one wall or bulletin board, give students a space to post pictures of themselves or news articles they find interesting. Not only will we get to know our students better, but they will make connections with each other as well.

• **Start an after-school club.** I used to run a baseball card collecting club after school, and many of my students signed up. We got to have lots of fun interactions that could not happen within the context of the regular school day.

• **Create a time capsule.** With students, collect artifacts and fun memories from your time together. Stash these all in a box and invite the students back a few years later for a reunion. Just knowing that they are going to be invited back allows students to see that you care about them beyond just this current year. You will feel great satisfaction when they come back to reminisce.

• **Post pictures of former classes.** This tip may seem counterintuitive. Shouldn't we post pictures of our current students? Yes, we should. Posting pictures of former students and classes also lends a sense of history to your classroom, showing students that they are important even after they leave.

Avoid Social Networking with Students

I was surprised one day when a 1st grader invited me to join her Facebook friends list. Here's an element of our profession that just did not exist a few years ago. While class Web sites, classroom blogs, and e-mail groups may be an important way for us to connect with students and families about our curricula, my suggestion is to not connect with students on social networking sites. It would just take one old college buddy to post a picture of you doing a keg-stand (I know, you never did such things in college, right?) for that picture to be out there for all students to see. So what was my response to the 1st grader? "I'd be happy to keep in touch by e-mail. Write me a note any time and I'll write back, but I don't connect with students on Facebook."

Building Relationships with Families

The other significant group of people with whom we work in schools are the families of our students. When parents or guardians know us and feel connected with us, they are more likely to be supportive of our efforts, offer us help when we need it, and approach problems with positive energy. When we feel connected to the families of our students, we feel a sense of belonging to the greater school community, which can help us better understand the culture of our students. It will also help us build a strong reputation in the parent community. Let's face it: ball field chatter matters. Parents talk with each other about their kids' teachers, and our jobs are a lot easier when parents come to us in the fall with a positive attitude.

Be Proactive

The more we can do at the beginning of the year to foster positive communication and make good connections with our students' families, the better. Invest some time and energy in proactive communication early in the year, and you will spend far less time on reactive communication later on. Here are some ideas for proactive communication:

• **Send a friendly letter home before the school year.** Introduce yourself. Tell about some of your experiences as a teacher (to build credibility) and some of your favorite hobbies and pastimes (to connect personally).

• **Hold an open house early.** If you can, invite families in to see your classroom and meet you before the year begins. Keep it loose and informal, simply a meet-and-greet.

• **Create a class Web site.** This site doesn't have to be fancy, just a place where parents can go to be reminded of upcoming events and see samples of class work.

• **Send notes home frequently.** A lot of short notes are more likely to be read and digested than a few lengthy letters. Take a little time to explain a new unit coming up or a new strategy you are trying. Parents will be understanding and supportive when they know that you are being thoughtful about your teaching.

• **Call home with good news.** In the first few weeks of school, call a few homes each night until you've personally connected with all of your families—a daunting task, but I encourage it nonetheless. Tell them a little something that has gone well, and let them know you are looking forward to a great year. Wouldn't we all like a call like that from our children's teacher?

• **Attend games and other student events.** When we head to the local ball field for a Little League game, when we attend the middle school band concert, or when we watch the school play, it gets noticed. We also get a chance to connect positively with the parents of students who are struggling academically or parents who may often shy away from discussions about schoolwork.

Respect the Teacher/Friend Boundary

Are you detecting a pattern here? Relationships are tricky things, ripe with potential and fraught with dangers. On the one hand, nurturing supportive and professional relationships with parents will help us better connect with our schools and better meet the needs of our students. Having close personal friends who are parents of our students can lead to conflicts of interest. Do we place their student differently with next year's teacher because of our friendship with their parents? Do students' grades change if they are on the edge of an *A-* and a *B+*? We also may pass along information about the dynamics of staff struggles to a good friend, a venting process that is natural and can help us process work-related stress, but what if that friend is also a parent at the school?

Belonging to the Greater Educational Community

One of the great things about being a teacher is that there are so many of us out there. With millions of teachers around the world, we have endless opportunities to connect with educators outside our own buildings.

Subscribe to a Publication

Whether it's a print or online publication, reading articles that pertain to your specific role in education lets you know that many people are struggling with the same issues. You are not alone! Consider writing a letter to the author of an article that really got you thinking. Such correspondence is much appreciated and can lead to ongoing professional dialogue. Once you have read a publication for a while, consider submitting an article for publication yourself. You will derive an immense sense of connection and belonging to the profession when others read and respond to your writing.

Connect with an Online Support Group

Creating or joining an educational blog can be a great way to network with a broad community of educators across the country and around the world. Many teachers are also connecting to teacher chat rooms and support groups using social networking tools such as Facebook. Like blogs, but often moderated or sponsored by a particular organization, these support groups can offer advice and ideas as well as serve as a forum for discussions and question-and-answer sessions. I talked with one educator who uses Twitter as a way of getting almost instant support. She'll post a quick question (e.g., "Help! What's a good way to help students connect with each other around Shakespeare?"), and within a few minutes, several people are chiming in with ideas.

Attend Conferences and Workshops

Workshops and conferences can be great places to connect with other teachers. I find that when I lead workshops, teachers often ask to get the e-mail addresses of the other participants because the relationships and dialogue that began are important to continue. Consider teaching a session at a conference for a chance to connect with other professionals in a different way.

Conclusion

A recent article in the *Washington Post* (Brown, 2009) illustrated the potential power of nurturing adult relationships in schools. Hybla Valley Elementary School in Fairfax County, Virginia, saw the percentage of students scoring in the proficient range in reading shoot from 68 percent to 85 percent and in math from 68 percent to 75 percent in just a few years after making a concerted effort to build both student-teacher and teacher-teacher relationships in the school.

Teaching is first and foremost about relationships: with our students, our colleagues, our administrators, parents, and others. A complex set of relationships and social needs are at play and are intertwined with all that we do. We can certainly teach in a school where we feel we do not belong. We can craft our lessons and feed them to disconnected students. We can sit next to colleagues at staff meetings and exchange shallow pleasantries. We can ignore the families of our students, hoping they will not appear at our door unhappy about something. We can smile at our principal and pray he will not come in for a visit. We can collect CEUs through in-district work so as to avoid taking workshops and not connect to others in the field. There's no doubt that we can do all of these things. But why would we? Teaching is such an all-consuming job that to not connect well with those around us is to neglect one of our most basic needs. Yes, we can teach without a sense of belonging, but I'll bet we won't last long—and we won't be very good while we do last.

One final note on taking the time to adopt some of the proactive strategies described in this chapter: A former colleague of mine always had a snappy comeback whenever I popped in to ask her a question. "Janie, do you have a minute?" I would begin. She would glance up at me quickly and with her tart southern accent say, "I do not *have* a minute, but for you I will *make* a minute." Her point is well taken. Fostering and maintaining professional and personal relationships with colleagues does take time, but it is time well spent. When we spend time nurturing relationships, both with colleagues and students at school as well as with parents and the greater educational community, we will feel more connected to our work and have more positive energy to pour into our teaching.

SPOTLIGHT ON A HEALTHY TEACHER

Jack, High School English Teacher

Jack has been teaching at his school for six years. When he first arrived, he was completely new to the area, having grown up and gone to college on the East Coast. Northern California was a shock at first. He immediately worked to build relationships at his school. An avid baseball fan, he offered to start a fantasy baseball league in his school, and he was thrilled when seven colleagues and an assistant principal took him up on his offer. Jack also developed a strong working relationship with a 6th grade team member, and they have been doing some collaborative projects for a couple of years now.

Building relationships with students has also been a priority for Jack. He tries hard to get to know all of his students, which is difficult because he works with all 120 6th graders on his team. He keeps a computer file for each class and spends a couple of minutes each day jotting notes about his students' academic and social interests and their growth. Though he designed this system to make sure that he really knew all of his students, a side benefit is that these notes have proved invaluable when talking with parents and attending IEP meetings. In addition, Jack is a part-time coach for the school's cross-country running club, which provides him with opportunities to connect with students outside of the classroom.

After five years of teaching, Jack was ready to connect with other high school English teachers, so he joined English Companion Ning. He checks in on this online community every day right after school and finds that it often inspires upcoming lessons and units. He has also begun to share stories and questions on the site, which is helping him feel connected to the broader educational community.

CHAPTER 4

Significance:
Teaching with a Sense of Purpose

Why did you enter the teaching profession? Perhaps you were inspired by an incredible teacher and wanted to make that same kind of positive impact on others. It may be that the reverse is true for you. I have talked with many teachers who had pretty rough experiences in school themselves and are committed to creating a more positive learning experience for children. You may be a career changer; you found yourself in a job or profession that did not seem meaningful, and you were looking for a way to make a broader impact on society. Like me, you may have simply discovered an aptitude for working with children and felt called to the profession, developing a sense of purpose and meaning along the way.

One of our most fundamental human needs is to have a sense of significance (Maslow, 1943). We need to know that our work is important and that we are having a positive influence on others, and this impact is one of the great strengths of our profession. As I interviewed teachers from all over the country and from a variety of school settings, this theme emerged time and time again: it is important to us that our work is meaningful. Having purpose in life is one of the things that help keep us going. When we feel the work we do has purpose beyond ourselves and that we are contributing to the greater good, we stay motivated and passionate about our work.

We in the educational community are pretty lucky. Teaching is widely regarded as one of the professions that has great purpose. In fact, over the course of my research to write this book, I spoke with many teachers who changed careers to become teachers, and they all cited their search for a profession with deeper meaning as what brought them to teaching. Consider the story of Bill Knittle, an elementary school teacher in Chester, Massachusetts.

Bill began working with newspapers in high school and college, first doing some writing and then working in advertising. He continued in journalism after college, landing a job at the *Hampton Gazette* (MA) before entering senior year. He worked in several newspapers over many years while getting married and raising his son. "I really enjoyed the work," he explained to me over lunch one day. His final position in this field was working as a general manager of a newspaper. He especially enjoyed this role because he got to work with editorials, which allowed him to help influence people.

Though Bill enjoyed working for newspapers, he had always wanted to be a teacher. Watching his 1st grade teacher, Mrs. Finton, he thought, "Wouldn't this be great? What a terrific job!" Every now and then, throughout his childhood and adulthood, thoughts of teaching would resurface. After his son graduated, he made the decision to get his master's degree and teaching certification. His student teaching experience and his first teaching job were in Sheffield Elementary School, run by Chip Wood, nationally known guru on education and cofounder of the Northeast Foundation for Children and author of the *Responsive Classroom*. Ruth Charney, fellow cofounder and author of *Teaching Children to Care* (2002), observed Bill several times and gave him feedback that first year.

Bill reports that he feels more vibrant, challenged, and passionate for his work than he had in his previous career. But for many of us, it can be shockingly easy to lose sight of our sense of purpose when we are mired in the daily minutiae of teaching. We begin the school year full of hopes, with our passion for teaching high. We cannot wait for students to arrive so we can get going on exciting projects and try out some new lessons and units we have been working on. Even the prospect of challenging students is exciting as we think about how rewarding it will be to make positive connections with them and get them excited about learning. Then we have that first union meeting where the union head is insulting the administration. That afternoon, we are reminded that we have six IEP files to review, and meetings will follow the next week. On the third day of school, we get a new student who does not speak English and requires a lot of extra support, and this happens to be the same day we get a phone call from a parent wondering why more challenging homework has not started coming home yet. Within a few weeks, it's easy to already feel disheartened and overwhelmed.

One of the most challenging aspects of being a teacher is that we must be able to see the forest and the trees at the same time. Hopeless visionaries who cannot manage the daily details of teaching do not last too long, but if we become unimaginative micromanagers, consumed by the daily challenges of school (e.g., meetings, little misbehaviors, collegial conflicts, standardized testing pressures, etc.), we quickly lose sight of the greater goals and aspirations that fuel our fire and drive us to be great teachers.

Let's examine some aspects of our career that relate to our sense of significance and explore them in depth. As in the other chapters of this book, we will try to minimize aspects that present challenges while being proactive and purposeful about how to hold on to a healthy sense of significance.

Noticing the "Little" Things

A high school history teacher greets students at the door as they enter class, and Jimmy, a normally quiet and reserved sophomore, sidles over to share a picture of his new puppy. A middle school math teacher is greeted with an enthusiastic smile and a wave from an energetic former student, even though she is traveling with a pack of friends. Nicky, a normally challenging 1st grader who often shoves and swears, quietly puts his hand into the hand of his teacher on the way out to recess.

Our hard work is recognized in a variety of other small ways throughout the year. Parents may write a nice note, thanking us for taking some extra time with their child. A colleague might tell us that he appreciated a comment that we made at a staff meeting. An administrator may send us a quick e-mail noticing something that our students have done well. These are actually not "little" things at all but important ways that people are showing us that our work matters and that we are significant. Instead of letting these seemingly small events roll off our backs, let's make sure to soak them up and cherish them. Here are a few specific ideas.

Collect Artifacts

I have a binder full of notes from parents and students thanking me or telling me that I made a difference. It used to be organized, but now it is a bit jumbled. That's okay. Just knowing it is there is comforting, and after a rough call from a parent who was upset (and leading me to feel less significant), I could open up the binder and remind myself that I was not a completely lost cause! If a binder is not your style, you could collect a digital scrapbook. Scan or take pictures of things that will remind you of your many successes. Even an old folder in the back of a file drawer could serve as an artifact repository. Here are just a few ideas of the kinds of artifacts we might collect:

- Notes from parents and students
- Newspaper articles highlighting your class or school
- Pictures of students you connected with
- Notes from colleagues/administrators
- List of committee work
- Updated résumé

Accept Compliments with Thanks

We will delve more deeply into this idea in the next chapter on competence. For now, consider believing students, parents, and colleagues when they tell you that you are making a difference. A high school teacher told me, "Teenagers can be so fickle and narcissistic. It's hard to take them seriously when they tell you you're their favorite teacher." To that, I say, "Believe it!" Whether we are really a kid's favorite teacher does not really matter. When students say something like that, we should just thank them and feel good. We are making a connection, and that's important.

Keep a Journal

Take five minutes at the end of each day to jot down some positive moments of the school day. Record the secret smile you got from a student during a read-aloud. Make a note about the student who passed the history test for which he had been studying so hard. This journal not only will turn into a nice collection of small yet significant events but also will train you to notice and remember such moments.

Setting Yourself Up for Significant Work in Your School

Here it is again—the importance of being proactive. Sure, kids, parents, colleagues, and administrators may all let us know how we are making a difference in our daily work, and it's important for us to recognize these things when they happen. But we can also do several things to set ourselves up for regular doses of significance.

Join a Committee and Work Toward a Cause

This might seem like odd advice, given the way most of us feel about committee work. I'm sure we have all had committee experiences that are about as fun as an unmedicated root canal. However, if there is a committee in your school or district for which you could get excited, sign up! What are you passionate about? What interests you about the larger school community? Whether you join the Green Team that will work toward recycling and composting or the negotiations team for your district's union, or co-chairing the PTO, there's nothing like fighting for something you believe in to boost your sense of significance.

Mentor or Coach a New Teacher

The opportunity to help a new colleague is exciting. If you are a veteran member of your school, you have a lot of knowledge and skills to share, both as a teacher and as someone who knows the ropes of your school. You'll find that the time and energy you spend will be more than paid back as you renew your own sense of purpose and focus on the bigger picture at school. If your school does not have an official mentoring program, you can still take a new staff member under your wing. Simply let her know she can come to you with any question. Remind him about the upcoming staff meeting or treat him to an occasional lunch.

Take On an Intern or Student Teacher

Having a prospective teacher working in your classroom can be a very rewarding experience. In addition to learning a lot yourself and making good connections with local colleges and universities, having an intern is a great way to contribute to the development of another professional. Sharing and teaching some of the good strategies we have developed helps boost our sense of significance. Having to explain what we do forces us to articulate our belief system and can help us further refine our own practice.

Become a Team Leader

Whether this form of leadership is an official role as the head of a high school department or an unofficial role as the go-to person on your 3rd grade team, being a leader and taking on some extra responsibility can be a great source of significance.

Be an Active Participant

Always sitting by and not asking a question or voicing an opinion at a staff meeting can lead you (and others) to believe that you do not have anything valuable to offer. You do! Share it.

Teach an After-School Activity

Do you enjoy knitting, scrapbooking, woodworking, or another hobby? If so, turn that hobby into an after-school class for either staff or students (or both). It is extremely satisfying to share our passions with others.

Offer a Workshop for Parents

Do you have some strategies that families could use to help with homework? Are parents in your school confused by new math or spelling instruction? These topics would be great miniworkshops to offer to any parent in the building.

Make Sure Not to Sell Yourself Short

Although doing more significant work in our schools can help boost our sense of significance in general, we need to be careful that we do not take on too many responsibilities without fair compensation. If we do, we may end up feeling unappreciated and undervalued, which could in fact diminish our sense of significance. For example, becoming part of a committee or helping facilitate a learning community in your school might be a great way to help shape the direction of your school community. Coaching a debate team, running an after-school reading program, or attending a professional workshop in the summer should all come along with compensation. Too often, out of a sense of responsibility, teachers give away too much time or spend their own money on things their schools should supply. We are setting ourselves up when we do this. Administrators and school boards may assume that these things do not require a line in the budget, knowing that teachers are willing to donate their time and resources. Before long, teachers are feeling like their time and efforts are not respected as they are asked to work too many hours with too few resources and without just compensation or funding.

Working Within the Broader Educational Community

In the previous chapter, I suggested that subscribing to a publication, joining an online community, and attending a conference are good ways to gain a greater sense of belonging to the educational community outside your own school. These same venues offer great opportunities to gain a greater sense of significance as well. Consider the following ideas:

• **Write a journal article.** I will never forget the thrill of having a research paper published. Greater yet was the day I got a response from a reader letting me know that the article had had an impact on her teaching.

• **Write for a blog or create your own.** I talked with one teacher who had started her own blog as a way of processing some of the things she was doing in her classroom. She was surprised to find that after a while, she had a small group of people reading her blog and responding. She knew she was making a difference with teachers in other schools.

• **Teach a workshop.** What is something that you are doing well that you could share? Perhaps you and a small team of colleagues could present some of your work at a local or national conference. It can be gratifying to know that when we share our successes with others, we are helping students in other places have a more successful school career.

Recognizing the Importance of Creativity and Teacher Voice

The past decade has seen an alarming trend in education. In an attempt to meet the demands of NCLB and the general move toward the standardization of curricula, many districts have adopted stale, cookie-cutter curricula. With lessons carefully scripted (and sometimes referred to as "teacher-proof"), these curricula are sapping teachers of creativity and voice.

I remember being handed a math program a few years back. Until that point, I had created my own math units and lessons to best fit the needs of my students while still delivering the content required by my district. It was exhausting putting together my own units and crafting my own lessons (which naturally changed each year based on the needs and strengths of my students), so I was intrigued by the thought of a curriculum where everything was mapped out. Just think of the time I'd save! And the homework was already there, prepackaged and ready to go!

I will admit that I did enjoy the decrease in planning time and the comfort of knowing that the math lessons, activities, and homework were already prepared each day. Interestingly enough, though, my enjoyment of teaching math waned the longer I used the program. The lessons did not always fit my students, and I was often confused by unfamiliar activities. Because I was not spending so much time creating units and lessons, I spent less time thinking about how (and why) to teach various aspects of math. Because the program spelled out exactly what I should do and how I should do it, I found my own interest in math dropping. I had lost my teacher voice in math. Not surprisingly, as my own sense of meaning and significance as a teacher decreased, my students felt disconnected from and uninterested in math as well.

In his essay "Stress, Control, and the Deprofessionalizing of Teaching," Tom Newkirk (2009) points out that studies have shown that workers who have less control of their work have higher rates of stress-related illnesses (e.g., high blood pressure, diabetes, and heart disease). He argues that one of the reasons teachers are feeling so much more stress in today's educational climate is that power and control are being stripped away from them via scripted curricula. An online comment that followed this article speaks to the truth of Newkirk's assessment: "This is exactly why I left the school I was in. The principal was buying Voyager for every subject and it is scripted and feels like Teaching for Dummies. I have a Masters Degree in Reading and over 20 yrs. of experience in teaching and it was so boring and insulting. I felt like I had no control over what was done in my classroom and no time to do what I knew was good for kids" (entry posted October 19, 2009).

Find Ways to Assert Your Voice and Get Creative

So, what do we do if we are handed a scripted program or curriculum? Resist! Fight back! Adjust and modify! Take that scripted math program and identify the good stuff tucked in there; then use that good stuff to enhance your own teaching. Take the science textbook—that dry, deadly, eight-pound monster—and use it as a resource and reference tool as you craft engaging and compelling units for your students. Take that stale essay writing unit and spruce it up. Make it fun. Change it around.

I know, I know. I can see some of you cringing at the very thought. "But my principal says that we're all supposed to be on the same page of the math program at the same time. She actually sends out reminders about the page we should be on!" I have heard this same sort of refrain from teachers all over the country. I like to counter with a question: have you ever heard of a teacher who was fired because she took a stale and dry curricular unit and made it better? It has probably happened somewhere, but I have yet to hear of an example. It seems to me that most principals have a hard enough time removing their *bad* teachers (the ones who sip coffee all day while handing out worksheets or the ones who beat the buses out of the parking lot every day). Why would they try to rid themselves of their good ones? I once heard a colleague at ASCD say, "It seems to me that the best teachers are the ones who are quietly rebellious." I think she is right on. It's okay for us to stand up for (and deliver) good teaching practices where we are putting the needs of our students above the needs of our curriculum.

Articulate an Ideal Vision

I was watching Ruth Charney, cofounder of Northeast Foundation for Children, teach an advanced workshop recently on the Responsive Classroom approach to teaching, and she challenged participants to think deeply about what they believed and what they wanted to create in their classrooms.

Now, I'd like to challenge you to do the same. Think about an aspect of your teaching. If you teach many subjects, choose one. It does not have to be a subject, though; it could be an element of teaching, such as direct instruction, conferring, or small-group work. Once you have chosen something on which to focus, write down exactly what this activity or quality would look like in action when done to perfection. What are you doing, and why are you doing it? What are students doing, and what is their motivation? Here are a couple of examples of what a vision statement like this might look like:

Vision for an Author Study Class Period
by Melanie, 8th Grade English Teacher

Students are each studying an author of their choice. Students are deeply engrossed in either a book they are reading or an analysis paper they are writing, detailing their understanding of various elements of plot, character development, setting, and recurring themes. While most of the class reads and writes, I am working at a table with a group of students who need a little extra coaching in symbolism. I have read an example, and they are scouring their texts for their own ideas. Two students in the corner of the room are having a peer conference to help each other with their analysis papers. The class has a collegial feel, and students are genuinely excited about their work. Though students in this class have a variety of reading levels, they are all examining texts that are appropriate for them, and they are feeling competent and valued. Though each student had to read (in class and for homework) at least three novels by the author they chose, many students have read more than this because they are so excited.

Vision for a Science Exploration

by Anthony, 1st Grade Teacher

As a class, we are studying the life cycle of insects. Students have been bringing in bugs all week long, and we've been collecting them in several terrariums throughout the class. This particular day, students are to choose one particular insect to study. They will draw the insect at least three times from three different perspectives. They will generate questions they have. They will also write down things they notice about their insect. Students will each get to examine their insect up close using magnifying glasses and minicontainers. Though the room is quite busy as students get colored pencils, jot down questions, and make loud exclamations ("Cool! I think I see the stinger on this bee!"), there is also a sense of studious attention as kids find energy in gathering information and asking new questions. As students work, I am circulating and working individually with students to help them add new ideas and think of new questions.

Articulating a clear vision can give you great energy. It forces you to set a goal that comes from your beliefs about what an ideal classroom should be. Instead of focusing on the content we must cover (generally not a great source of significance), we focus on what we should do and why it is important (a great source of significance).

Craft a Philosophical Statement

According to Patricia Houghton (2001), teachers who are allowed to teach according to their own beliefs are happier. What do you believe about teaching and learning? To help yourself focus on the bigger picture, try crafting a philosophical statement. More broad and general than a vision for an ideal moment, a philosophical statement is an overarching description of your professional belief system. Too often in teaching, we get caught up in *what* we teach and *how* we teach it. Every now and then, we need to dig deeper and examine *why* we teach and why we do what we do.

When crafting a philosophical statement, consider the following questions as a starting point. You might focus on just one or attempt to address several in one statement:

- What are your core beliefs about how students learn?
- What is the ideal learning environment?
- Why did you choose to go into teaching?
- How does a good education improve society?
- What were some of your most important experiences as a student, and how have they shaped who you are as a teacher?

Put Together a Professional Portfolio

Creating and maintaining a professional portfolio is another way we can focus on ways we are significant at school. Often we are making a real impact, but we fail to notice all of the important ways we contribute to our schools. Creating a professional portfolio encourages us to collect and celebrate things that we have done that have made an impact. A portfolio could be a three-ring binder with written statements and artifacts from our teaching, or it could be an online presentation that links to photo galleries and videos. Whatever format you use, consider some of the following ideas:

- Include belief and vision statements.
- Collect artifacts from your work with students, parents, colleagues, and others.
- Focus on work samples that show how you have affected others.
- Include notes and cards from students and their families.
- Brush up your résumé!

Recognize the Impact of Societal Perceptions on Our Sense of Significance

Both positive and negative perceptions of teachers and teaching are floating around out there. Politicians regularly pander to teachers in stump speeches, praising us for entering such a noble profession, but limited governmental funding for public education sends a different message about how society values what we do. The national debate about No Child Left Behind and the ensuing labeling of schools as "failing" have demoralized educators across the country. As I heard one teacher say, "For years, we wished that the federal government would step in and get more active in education. Now we wish they'd just go away." We all probably have some friends or family members who are both openly supportive and openly critical of teachers. Many teachers told me that they felt disheartened by bad press or other negative perceptions of our profession. Now, this book is focused on what we can do to better take care of ourselves, so it may seem odd to spend time discussing how people outside education view us, but let's face it: if our sense of significance as teachers is in part met (or not met) by how our profession is viewed, then it's up to us to see if we can improve that perception. Doing so will not only help us in the short term but also be good for our profession in the long term. So, let's examine a few ways that we can tackle some of these societal perceptions, especially in our own schools and districts.

Consider How We Present Ourselves to Parents and Community Members

According to a recent Phi Delta Kappa/Gallup poll (Bushaw & McNee, 2009), school employees were the second-most important source of information for people about their town's public schools. The way we present ourselves to the public can have a major impact on how our schools are viewed.

Imagine being a parent and walking into a school. You are trying to find a conference room where you have a team meeting scheduled to review your son's IEP. One of the two following scenes ensues. How will it affect your views about teachers and schools?

School 1

You walk into the school and begin to walk down the hall, looking for the conference room. The gray-green walls are tastefully decorated with student artwork and writing pieces. A display case nearby shows 3-D projects from a recent science unit. A teacher is walking by. Dressed in a pencil skirt and sharp blouse, she immediately smiles at you. "Can I help you?" she asks.

School 2

You walk into the school and begin to walk down the hall, looking for the conference room. The industrial off-white paint on the walls is peeling, and bulletin boards with notices and schedules are messy and crooked. A teacher is walking by. Dressed in jeans and a sweatshirt, she shuffles by quickly with a sour expression, her head buried in a pile of papers. She doesn't make eye contact.

We can do so many little things to make a good impression on visitors to our schools. Friendly and open office staff, clean hallways, and tasteful landscaping can all make a difference. Here are some specific suggestions for helping people see your school as a professional and inviting place.

• **Dress professionally.** Consider business-casual dress. When we dress professionally, we send a message that we are professional. Matters of appearance may seem superficial to some (I argued that very thing at the beginning of my career), but consider how you would feel if you showed up at your doctor's office to see your doctor dressed as if he were about to do some yard work. How would his appearance affect your opinion of the quality of his work?

• **Greet visitors and see how you can help.** Saying hello is more than just a common courtesy. When people are greeted in a friendly way, they feel welcomed and are inclined to be positive about your school.

• **Pay attention to your body language.** One of the first things I notice about a school when I arrive is the body language of staff in the office and in the hallways. Good posture, friendly faces, and relaxed arms indicate a building where people feel comfortable, confident, and energized. Furrowed brows, crossed arms, hurried walking, slouching, and shuffling give the impression of people who feel fearful, tired, and stressed.

Be Proactive About Local Media Coverage

If school employees are the second-most important source of information for people about their town's public schools, what's the first? Local newspapers. Many teachers I spoke with voiced frustration at their local newspaper's negative coverage of the public schools in their town. One teacher in New Hampshire said that he felt that any hint of a drug issue or a fight at the high school seemed to earn front-page status at the local paper. Sadly, scandals probably sell more newspapers or attract more TV viewers than stories about fun projects or academic successes. That being said, I think schools usually do a pretty poor job of communicating good news to local media.

Be proactive! For example, set up a liaison with your local newspaper—a staff member who calls the paper once a week to feed information about exciting field trips, science fairs, and interesting classroom projects. In one school in which I worked, the school secretary would periodically put out a notice for staff members to feed her ideas for good stories to our local newspaper. As a result, we had more positive coverage in our newspaper (Bushaw & McNee, 2009).

Do Not Take Yourself Too Seriously

Of the major categories outlined in this book so far, significance may be the one most built into our profession. We are teachers because we want to make a difference. The work we do is important.

A danger here is that we can take ourselves too seriously. We can overdo our own sense of significance so that it becomes a hindrance to good health instead of an asset. Consider the following examples:

Jerry's Challenge: "The kids can't live without me"

Jerry is an outstanding teacher in a tough urban school. Crime is rampant, and the kids are needy. Many students in Jerry's science classes tell him that he is their favorite teacher, and he knows that many of them behave much better in his class than they do in his colleagues' classes. Jerry is passionate about the importance of good science education and sees the work he does as a potential ticket to a better life for his students. Because of his deep belief in the good work he is doing and his fear of what might happen if he is not there, Jerry refuses to take a sick day. There are some days when he comes to school with a fever, and other days when he is emotionally and physically exhausted and would benefit from a day at home to rest and recover.

Mike's Challenge: "I know what's best for my kids"

Mike has a strong set of beliefs about the right way to teach. Each year, his 4th graders learn a lot and enjoy school. He has a system that works for him, and he has become rigidly attached to the idea that he knows what's best for his kids. When his grade-level team wants to try something new, his first inclination is to resent the idea that there might be a better way to teach. When his principal wants to explore a new literacy program, Mike immediately reacts negatively. "I know what works for my kids," he contends. Unable to see the bigger picture and unwilling to listen to others' points of view, Mike becomes stuck in a mode of teaching that is indeed successful but, more important to his sense of significance, also too rigid and safe.

Sarah's Challenge: "I'm not significant if I'm not overworked"

As a middle school English teacher, Sarah has a lot of paperwork. Daily homework assignments, coupled with essays and longer papers, require her to spend long hours after school assessing, offering feedback, and grading. Though she has not admitted this truth to herself, a part of her relishes being the archetype of the overworked teacher. When friends call her up and ask her to come over for pizza on a Thursday night, she secretly enjoys their reply to her denial: "Sarah! You work too hard!" "I know," she replies. "Being a teacher is really tough."

All three of these stories illustrate one of the dangers of our profession. Teachers don't just teach. We *are* teachers. Teaching is how we identify ourselves. In our society, which places a huge emphasis on what we do for a living to determine our value as people, we proudly say, "I am a teacher." This pride, this sense of significance about our work, is justified, but it can also allow us to take ourselves too seriously. So, for the Jerrys out there: Sure, our class may be out of control when we are not there, but we still need to take care of ourselves. We will be better teachers if we stay home with a fever or take an occasional mental health day to regain our strength and spirit. For all of the Mikes out there: Don't get so caught up in the idea that you are a good person *because* you are a good teacher. Loosen up a little and be open to new ideas. Good teachers are good learners. And for poor Sarah and all of us like her: It's not the amount of work that makes us a good teacher but the quality. Beware of playing the part of the martyr—martyrs must die, after all. Instead, create assignments that are still meaningful without requiring hours of work each night on your end. As explored in depth in the next chapter, we can be good without killing ourselves in the process.

Conclusion

In this chapter, we have looked at how to meet our needs for significance at school, but let's not forget to take care of those needs outside school, too. As described in Chapter 7 on balance, we need to work at satisfying all of our needs outside school so that when we hit a downturn at work, we have some reserves in other places. Work with a church youth group. Coach a soccer team. Spend time volunteering at a nursing home. Chip in at your local food bank. Spend time with your family and friends.

Maintaining meaningful connections outside work can help us keep our perspective healthy at school. After a rough staff meeting, a dispiriting day with students, or a challenging interaction with a parent, we can come home and remember that there is more to life than teaching. This sense of significance can allow us to disconnect from school, refocus on other ways in which we are important and make a difference, and give us the emotional recharging time that we need so that we can shake off the bad day at school and get in a positive frame of mind for the next.

SPOTLIGHT ON A HEALTHY TEACHER

Suzanne, Middle School Music Teacher

Suzanne teaches music in a midsized middle school. She has always loved music and truly enjoys adolescents, and she sometimes feels like her job was created just for her. In the beginning of her career, however, she struggled with maintaining a strong sense of significance. Colleagues did not always understand how hard it is to work with so many different students when you see them only once a week. Parents sometimes questioned her grading practices and made it clear that music was not really all that important. Whenever the local school board contemplated budget cuts, the music program seemed to always be at the top of the list. There were days she went home feeling defeated.

At the suggestion of a colleague, Suzanne began keeping a scrapbook. One of the advantages of being a music teacher is that you tend to get more positive coverage in the local newspapers. Every time she directed a holiday concert or had former students from the high school featured in an article, she clipped it and saved it. She also collected nice notes from students and parents.

Suzanne also decided to be a little more proactive with her colleagues. Every now and then, she passed along an article she read about connections between music and other academic areas. She offered to collaborate with a science teacher who was crafting a unit on sound. The collaboration went well, and other teachers started to ask if she would be interested in working together.

Many staff members now recognize Suzanne as a leader in the school. When it was time to hire a new art teacher, her principal asked Suzanne if she would serve on the hiring committee. The next time a budget cut looms, Suzanne will be ready. She has been collecting research about the positive impacts of a music program on middle school students and is ready to make her case.

CHAPTER 5

Competence:
The Importance of Self-Efficacy

The secret of joy in work is contained in one word—excellence.
To know how to do something well is to enjoy it.

Pearl S. Buck

We need to know that we are good at what we do. Just about every article and essay I read as I researched this book that dealt with feeling good about the workplace asserted that in order to really like the work we do, we have to feel competent. This makes sense. Success breeds motivation. When we know we are good at what we do, we are excited to work at it some more and have greater positive energy for our work.

Of all the information I collected, the simple idea that we have to know that we are good at teaching in order to fully enjoy it was perhaps the greatest "A-ha!" (as well as the greatest "Well, duh!") moment of my research. This perhaps is no great revelation in general. We know that our students are more motivated by their successes than by their failures. My daughter, who is now six, is spending incredible amounts of time working at learning to read at home because things are really clicking. Within the last few months, her sight word vocabulary, her understanding of how words are constructed, and her ability to recognize key letter combinations and their sounds have all increased dramatically. As she gains greater confidence in her reading abilities, working at reading becomes more fun, so she reads more.

The revelation came not in the idea itself but in the realization that so many teachers struggle with a sense of competence in their own teaching. I think that many teachers feel incompetent—which is ironic, because I think the vast majority of teachers are more than competent. Most teachers I know are talented, articulate, thoughtful, hardworking professionals. We lead 20-plus students, each with different needs and strengths, through the daily explorations of math, science, social studies, literacy, and social skills. We model patience and caring. We negotiate the needs and demands of families, administrators, and colleagues even when they do not match our own personal goals and belief systems. We have incredible management, social, and organizational skills. Despite all of our skills and talents, however, we still can feel like we do not measure up. A former colleague comes to mind.

> Jean was a highly respected 5th grade teacher, admired by students, parents, and colleagues. Organized, kind, and smart, she had many qualities of a great teacher. She spent big blocks of time preparing lessons and units. Each year, some of the neediest students in the grade ended up in her room because everyone knew that she could make a huge impact on them. But somehow, Jean did not see herself the way everyone else did. She often spoke of her own teaching in self-critical ways: "I'm such a terrible math teacher"; "I don't think I can learn this new science unit well enough." She often got highly defensive and nervous at staff meetings, sometimes breaking down in tears when feeling threatened. One year, our principal was toying with the idea of opening up choice to parents about where their children would be placed for the upcoming year, and Jean was paralyzed by fear. This expert and highly regarded teacher cried out, "What if no one wants to be in my class?" Even though Jean was a highly skilled teacher with a great reputation who worked really well with children, she wasn't very happy as a teacher. She *was* good; she just didn't *think* she was good.

Jean may seem like an extreme example, but I have seen hundreds of teachers gripped with these same kinds of insecurities. And when teachers are insecure, it's hard for them to feel confident enough to try new strategies and take healthy risks. I am not contending that we should never question our own teaching practices. In fact, I think it's a healthy thing for all of us to question what we do and come up with ways we can get better. Later in this chapter, we'll explore the importance of effective goal setting, because seeing ways we can get better is an important way we can boost our sense of competence. Let's just make sure that we keep a healthy balance between looking for ways to improve and noticing and celebrating what we are doing well.

How Does Competence Differ from Significance?

As I first began drafting this book, competence was simply a subheading under significance, but the more I worked with these ideas, the more things didn't seem to quite fit. We gain a sense of significance from how we affect others, and an important part of that is their recognition of our impact. When a student or a parent thanks us for a great year, we feel significant. When we help write a curricular unit or help shape school goals through committee work, we see ways in which we have made an impact on others. Our sense of competence, however, has more to do with our own view than of others' view of us. In fact, if we are relying on others to tell us how good we are to feel good about our teaching, we are probably in trouble because administrators are often too busy to give us great feedback about our teaching, and colleagues rarely actually watch us teach. If we are going to feel good about our teaching, we must explore ways to take care of this need ourselves. The rest of this chapter offers various strategies for doing just that.

Research on Self-Efficacy

Not surprisingly, the research on teacher efficacy bears out the importance of having a strong sense of competence. An essay by Megan Tschannen-Moran and Anita Woolfolk Hoy (2001) summarizes multiple studies that show the results of high teacher self-efficacy (the confidence teachers have in their teaching and their ability to meet professional challenges). It shows that when teachers have a high degree of self-efficacy, they are more persistent, work harder, have more enthusiasm for teaching, are less critical of students who make errors, have more goals and aspirations, are more open to new ideas, and have a greater commitment to teaching.

An example from my own work with teachers comes to mind. I had been coaching a few teachers for a couple of years when it struck me that they seemed more relaxed and joyful than they had been a year earlier. They were still having rich and interesting discussions about their students and their teaching, but there just did not seem to be the level of anxiety that I had seen before. This change was especially interesting as one of them had told me that she had a much more difficult class this year than she had the previous year. "You all seem so much more relaxed than this time last year. What's the difference?" I asked. Their responses were interesting. "Oh," began one, "I still have days where I'm tearing my hair out." Another chimed in: "There's one student in my room this year who's really tough. She can drive me crazy some days." The first teacher nodded and continued. "I think last year I didn't even know what was wrong when things weren't going well in my classroom. This year, I not only know what's wrong, but I've got some ideas that I know I can try." A third teacher laughed, "And even when I make a mistake, I know I made the mistake and know what I'll do differently next year."

The simple fact that these teachers have learned some new strategies that they know can help them in their classrooms has made them more confident in their ability to tackle challenges. They are under no illusion that they have all the answers and will never have any more challenges, but they know they have some tools to use. They are happier and more relaxed as a result.

If we know we are effective, we have a better chance of being happy and healthy at school. When we are happy and healthy at school, we have a better chance of having positive energy and greater engagement in our work. Once again, though this chapter is about how we can better take care of ourselves, our students will also benefit.

Some Key Mind-Set Shifts

It's important to recognize factors that may hinder our chances of feeling a greater sense of competence. Let's take a good look at some of these roadblocks to self-efficacy and explore some strategies for overcoming them.

Become Less Dependent on Others' Approval

Researchers such as Alfie Kohn (1993) have outlined the negative out-comes of growing up in a society in which children are praised or shamed for their behavior. An overreliance on others' feedback for our own sense of self-worth is a common outcome. Especially for younger teachers, this depen-dency can be a great challenge. Jeffery Zaslow (2007) has documented how younger workers (across the workplace, not just in teaching) are requiring more and more praise to stay motivated to work. Having been raised as praise junkies, many workers seem to be unable to feel validated unless someone is constantly telling them how great they are. The article goes on to outline how some companies are going to ridiculous lengths to stroke their workers, such as throwing confetti and handing out helium balloons to workers, hiring "cel-ebration assistants" to heap praise on employees, and sending out a barrage of e-mail acknowledgments throughout the day.

This need to be recognized by others can be crippling, especially in a pro-fession where the fruits of our work are often intangible and where peer feed-back does not come naturally. If we are totally hooked into looking to others for our sense of self-worth, it can be awfully hard to self-assess. How do we examine our own practice and determine whether what we are doing is good enough? Another challenge for teachers in this area is that many of us are still so isolated. If we are only going to be able to feel good about the science lesson we just taught if someone else pays us a compliment about it, we are pretty unlikely to feel that way because our colleagues and administrators are probably not watching. Another problem with this dependence on praise is that if we believe people should praise us when we are doing well, simple silence, or an absence of praise, can feel like criticism.

This point brings us to supervision and evaluation. When was the last time you had meaningful feedback from an administrator in your building? As I mentioned earlier in my 15 years in the classroom, I was officially observed by my principal three times. Administrators are just as overworked and stressed out—maybe even more so—as teachers, so it's hard for them to get into class-rooms to give meaningful feedback and coaching to teachers, especially the ones who they think are doing well.

Herein lies a paradox. Several teachers told me that they wish they got more recognition and positive feedback from their principal, yet just as many seemed to have a crushing fear of being observed. So here we have a system where many teachers do not feel good about their teaching unless they are being complimented by others, but they do not actually want anyone watching them teach!

If you are struggling with a dependence on others for positive feedback, the following ideas might help you combat these feelings of insecurity:

• **Buddy up with a colleague.** Find a colleague and take turns visiting in each other's classrooms. Make a point of finding specific positives that you see in each other's classes and recognize those with each other.

• **Invite your principal in for an informal visit.** If you have a cool project going on or would simply like some feedback on a lesson, invite your principal to visit. Some administrators would like to be in classrooms more often but do not want to seem obtrusive or overbearing. Most principals love to be asked to drop in.

• **Begin to self-assess more often.** Examine your own practice to identify things you do well. Later in this chapter we'll look at how to set good goals and observe our practice objectively.

Believe It's Okay to Be Proud of Yourself

Another roadblock to our ability to feeling a great sense of competence is our fear of appearing prideful. Let's try a simple exercise to see if this is true. Say the following statement out loud: "I'm proud to be a teacher." Easy enough? Does that roll right off your tongue? Have you said that before? Now try saying this statement: "I'm proud of *my teaching*." How did that go? Did you feel a bit embarrassed, like you should not actually verbalize that sentiment? Have you said that phrase as often as the first? Why is it so easy for many of us to express pride in our profession but not in ourselves?

I think that reluctance often has to do with the culture of our schools. My own experience certainly bears this out, and many teachers I interviewed have felt the same way. All too often, an unwritten commandment exists in schools: "Though shalt not appear to outdo thy neighbor." Whether it is really true or not is almost irrelevant. Most teachers' perception of their schools' culture is that it is not safe to appear proud of their work because others might think that they believe they are better than their peers.

Let's think back to our previous discussion of some teachers' need to be praised. Have you ever noticed how difficult it is for so many teachers to accept a compliment? Here are a couple of typical conversations between two colleagues, one of whom is complimenting the other:

Teacher 1: Wow! I was watching your kids at the assembly yesterday. They were so quiet and respectful! You must have really worked hard with them on that.

Teacher 2: Oh, that was just a good day. You should have seen them when there was a substitute in the day before.

Teacher 1: Thanks for letting me observe your math lesson yesterday. Your lesson was so clear and direct.

Teacher 2: Yeah, but some kids still didn't get it. It could have been better.

Some of us (including me for a long time) have both sets of baggage to deal with. On the one hand, we are dying for someone, *anyone*, to pay us a compliment and notice our good work; on the other hand, we are ready to deflect any and all compliments when they happen, afraid of appearing cocky or boastful.

The following ideas are a few ways we might combat this fear of being prideful:

• **Eliminate negative self-talk.** Be careful not to engage in lots of self-deprecating talk about your own teaching. You know what I mean: "I'm really not very good at math, but ..." or "I'm not the best writer, but ...." This self-deprecation is far too easy a habit to fall into, and the danger is that we may actually come to believe ourselves.

• **When complimented, say, "Thank you."** And that's it! Instead of deflecting the compliment, even if you feel like it may be off-base, just accept it with thanks. Allow yourself to feel good that someone else noticed you doing something well.

• **Give yourself permission to feel good.** Each day contains some things that go well. Make sure that you pick out a few good moments from each day and allow yourself to feel good about them.

Focus on What You *Can* Control

Many teachers focus their energy on things they cannot control. Homework is a classic example. I remember spending hours of my time and energy trying to come up with strategies and solutions for my 5th grade students who were not getting their homework assignments done. The more I tried, the more I felt like an absolute failure. It was a blessed day when I finally realized that I could not control whether they did their homework or not. I could teach them good homework strategies. I could assign work that they could do independently. I could even give them my phone number so they could call me for help if they needed it. But in the end, they were the ones who were ultimately responsible for doing the work; and if they did not do it, that was their deal, not mine.

As we touched on in the previous chapter, the less control we have over our profession, the greater levels of stress we experience. An article in *British Educational Leadership* notes, "Psychologists and other stress analysts have discovered that the most trying professions are those that involved high pressure and serious responsibilities, often beyond the control of the individuals employed" (Sorenson, 2007, p. 10). Another study found that as teachers have more control over their curricula, their on-the-job stress decreases. It also showed that as teacher autonomy increases, teachers have a greater sense of empowerment and professionalism (Pearson & Moomaw, 2005).

There are so many aspects of our teaching that we can control. And there are so many that we cannot. For example, we can control the tone of voice that we use with students, but we cannot control the way our colleagues speak. We can control the way we use resources in our classrooms, but we do not have much say in the budget process.

Consider some of the aspects of school that stress you out and make you feel disheartened. Which ones can you control? Focus on those. Which ones are outside your control? Let those go. Do not spend time and energy on things that you cannot change. The list in Figure 5.1 may be a useful starting point, but consider adding to it with examples from your own experience.

Figure 5.1 Focus on What We Can Control	
Things we often can control	**Things we often cannot control**
• Our tone of voice • The structure of lessons we teach • How we communicate with parents • The discipline system we employ • The homework we assign • The arrangement of the classroom furniture	• Scheduling • School homework policy • Parents • Colleagues • High-stakes testing • Our school's resources • Class size

Granted, an argument could be made that we *do* in fact have some control over all of the items in the right-hand column of Figure 5.1. We can have an impact on scheduling and homework policies through committee work and communication with administration, we can fight against NCLB through calling members of Congress and writing editorials in our local papers, and so forth. In fact, I think it would be great to work at changing some of the larger issues that make teaching so challenging. My caution is not to take on some of these bigger issues as reasons why we cannot feel competent. While fighting on a grander scale for smaller class sizes is a noble pursuit, we still need to find ways to see ourselves as competent with our English class of 30 sophomores.

What Does It Mean to Be a Good Teacher? The Importance of Appropriate Goal Setting

Isn't it interesting that as an educational community, we cannot reach any real consensus about what it means to be a good teacher? Is it someone who is rigorous and pushes her students unbelievably hard? Is it someone whom the kids and parents all love? Is it someone who integrates technology (or art or music or movement) into his teaching? Is it someone who always finishes the curricular objectives for the year? At one school where I taught, the only kind of public teacher recognition went to teachers who endured the whole year without taking a sick day, so maybe a good teacher is simply someone who shows up to school reliably. Or, perhaps we adhere to that old colloquial adage: we cannot define a good teacher, but we know one when we see one.

It's telling that the Bill and Melinda Gates Foundation set aside $45 million to study how to measure teacher effectiveness (Anderson, 2009). Our profession is so complex and with so many ways to measure our effectiveness, narrowing down what defines a good teacher can be overwhelming.

So, let's start to explore how we can actually get better, because *feeling* better about ourselves as teachers is vitally important, but if that perception is not grounded in reality, it will not do our students nearly as much good. Let's also acknowledge that many books and resources are available on how to improve our teaching (e.g., Danielson, 1996), and that topic is not a major focus of this book. Instead, we are going to explore one particular skill that can help all of us, regardless of whether we teach high school physics, middle school art, or self-contained first grade: good goal setting.

First, it's important to make sure we are clear about what kind of goal setting we mean here. We are talking about clear, meaningful, observable goals—ones that we know will matter to us and our students, versus the often stale, bland, and forced goal setting of a supervision and evaluation meeting—you know, the one where an administrator makes you come up with a goal for the next year. We dutifully type up the form, usually putting down some goal that we were probably going to work on anyway (or that we already do—let's be honest) that can't really be measured easily (e.g., "My goal is to make science lessons more inquiry based so that students have more academic engagement"). I myself never found these kinds of goal-setting activities particularly useful and could never remember what my official professional goal for a year was come December.

We are also not talking about goals handed to us from somebody else based on district plans or standardized test results. Again, I have found that these goals can have a limited practical use. Goals of this kind are often based on previous year's data from different children who may or may not have similar learning needs as our current students. These kinds of goals are often meant to apply to a large set of teachers with varying skill sets and needs, so the goals set by the district may or may not apply to what we personally need to work on to get better as a teacher.

The goal setting I am talking about here has to do with the everyday, on-the-spot, real-life, and meaningful goal setting that we should be doing on our own in the course of trying to best reach our students and improve our own skill sets. It often happens quickly and does not need to involve immense amounts of paperwork, professional conferences, or lots of time. In the following section, we will explore how to observe our students and collect data in order to set specific and meaningful goals for our teaching.

All too often, teachers' goals tend to be vague and fuzzy. "I want to be the best teacher I can be" is one I've heard a lot. Another common one is "I'm going to try my best." You might be wondering what the problem is with wanting to try our best or be the best we can be. Aren't these noble goals?

The problem with these goals is that they are undefined, impossible to measure, and impossible to achieve. What do we really mean when we say we want to "be the best teacher we can be" or even "try our best"? What does that look like? What will we do to move closer to attaining these goals? More important, *can* we attain these goals? I would argue that we cannot. No matter how hard we try or how well we do, we can always find ways things could have gone better, so setting a goal of "being our best" or "trying our best" is guaranteeing failure. Another former colleague comes to mind.

Cathy teaches 1st grade. One morning before school, we were having breakfast at a local diner and discussing our classes. Cathy was feeling really frustrated. She felt like she could not meet the individual needs of all of the children in her class. She expressed a sense of failure because she felt like no matter how hard she tried, her best was not good enough. Then she stopped and chuckled, rolled her eyes, and said, "I just want to be the best teacher I can be, but of course if I had just one kid and had them 24/7, I still wouldn't be able to meet all of his needs. My best still wouldn't be good enough."

Whoa. This is a teacher whom all of the kids in the school adore, whether they had her in 1st grade or not. That year, she coordinated a year-long Destination Imagination season that involved nearly 20 percent of the student population of our school. She had only 14 students in her class and had other full-time adult support for her students. She is a veteran teacher of 15 years yet still has the youthful appearance, energy, and passion of a new teacher, and she is widely admired by her colleagues. She puts in more hours than most and is often in school on the weekends, planning creative and innovative ways to challenge and excite her students. Yet like many of us, she feels that she is not good enough. She often speaks of her teaching in self-deprecating ways and sees herself as not doing her job well enough.

By all reasonable accounts, Cathy is an enormously successful teacher, yet she sees herself as a failure. This vague goal of being the best teacher she can be is doing her no good at all, and I think she is typical of many teachers out there. With mushy, unattainable goals, it's hard for us to have a strong sense of self-efficacy.

Setting Practical Goals

So, how do we set good goals—ones that will help us get better and help us see our successes clearly? We can use a simple process based on the same kind of learning cycle that we encourage students to use in science: (1) observe and collect data, (2) examine data and generate ideas, (3) choose a goal (4) assess through observation and data collection, and (5) consider next steps. Let's examine each of these steps.

1. Observe and collect data. After a lesson, at the end of the day, or at the end of a unit, we reflect on what went well and what could have been better and begin to make plans for adjustments and changes. "Hmm, I noticed that students really seemed to understand the Pythagorean theorem when they were in small groups, but then when they went to try it on their own, many of them really struggled." Or "The class was so quiet and focused before lunch, but when they came back from recess, they were so wound up that they couldn't focus on the science lesson." These kinds of observations are a great starting point for a possible new goal. We have noticed something that could use some improvement, and then questions inevitably arise: "Do students see things the same way I do? Are my hunches on target? How many students are exhibiting what I think I'm seeing?" Now it's time to collect some data to bring our observations beyond the "I think I'm noticing …" point. The most helpful data are often the kind that can be gathered simply and quickly. Figure 5.2 describes a few examples.

Figure 5.2	Data Collection	
Observation	**Question(s)**	**Data Collection**
Students seem confused about a new math concept.	Are they really confused? How many students are struggling? What do they need help with?	**Quick Quiz:** "Hey, everyone! We're going to have a quick quiz so that I can better understand what I need to teach next to help you master this new concept."
Students seem a bit squirrelly at a certain time of the day.	How many students are "wired" at that time? Are there other times when it is also like that?	**Tally Chart:** Keep a clipboard handy. Several times a day, spend a few minutes tallying up the number of times the behavior is exhibited.
Students are grumbling about a new unit.	Are they upset about the content? Do they have some good ideas for how to make it better? Do they have some valid complaints?	**Class Discussion:** Take 10 minutes at the end of a period to check in with the class. "I've heard some grumbling the last couple of days. I'm wondering what's up."
You have the sense that your lessons are going too long. Students seem to be losing their focus at the end.	How long is the lesson going, really? How long are students maintaining their focus?	**Stopwatch:** Time the lesson. Note when students seem to start drifting.

2. Examine data and generate ideas. Once we have noticed a problem, collected some data, and fleshed out a few questions, we can move on to the next step, which is to look at the results of the data and come up with a few ideas for how we can work on the problem. Then we can set some specific and measurable goals for tackling it (Figure 5.3).

3. Choose a goal. Now that we have some ideas, we can choose one that seems likely to work and give it a try.

4. Assess through observation and data collection. When we try our new idea, we must collect more data by observing our students so that we can determine whether it worked (Figure 5.4). This step may be the most important part of the whole process, because it is where we get to boost our sense of efficacy.

5. Consider next steps. How did things turn out? What next steps might be necessary?

Figure 5.3	Examine Data and Generate Ideas	
Data Collection	**The Data Show ...**	**Possible Goals to Try**
Quick Quiz: "Hey, everyone! We're going to have a quick quiz so that I can better understand what I need to teach next to help you master this new concept."	Half the class did not understand the concept at all, and another 5 students had only minimal understanding. Four students fully understood the concept.	1. I could reteach the lesson to the whole class. 2. I could use the students who did understand the concept and ask them to help the other students who did not understand the lesson. Each student who mastered the content could teach a group of four students while I circulate and coach.
Tally Chart: Keep a clipboard handy. Several times a day, spend a few minutes tallying up the number of times the behavior is exhibited.	After lunch *is* a tough time. Sixteen of the 23 students were using loud voices or shoving through the door. Five students were especially rough.	1. I could have the class line up outside the classroom when they return from lunch. I could then send them in five at a time. 2. I could reteach and model how to enter the classroom appropriately after lunch.
Class Discussion: Take 10 minutes at the end of a period to check in with the class. "I've heard some grumbling the last couple of days. I'm wondering what's up."	Students aren't interested in the new unit. They do not see why they have to learn it. They also do not understand some of the big ideas.	1. I could let students choose some mini-research projects within the larger unit. 2. I could connect the main themes to their lives. 3. I could structure a debate about some of the key ideas.
Stopwatch: Time the lesson. Note when students seem to start drifting.	My main lesson was 25 minutes. A couple of students started to drift at 8 minutes. About half the class was losing focus at 12 minutes.	1. I will keep my main lesson to a maximum of 10 minutes. 2. We will do a movement activity right before the lesson starts.

Figure 5.4	Assess Results and Determine Next Steps		
Ideas to Try	**Choose One Goal**	**Collect Data and Examine Results**	**Next Steps**
1. I could reteach the lesson to the whole class. 2. I could use the students who did understand the concept and ask them to help the other students who did not understand the lesson. Each student who mastered the content could teach a group of four students while I circulate and coach.	I'll split the class into four groups, with a student who understands the content heading up each group.	**Quick Quiz:** The second quiz showed improved scores. This time, 12 students showed mastery and only 2 were still really struggling.	I'll work with these two students on my own. I'll consider using this small-group coaching model again.
1. I could have the class line up outside the classroom when they return from lunch. I could then send them in five at a time. 2. I could reteach and model how to enter the classroom appropriately after lunch.	I'll model (again) how to re-enter the class after lunch.	**Tally Chart:** Twelve students continued to be wild when entering the room.	Tomorrow I'm going to have the class line up outside the door, and I'll send them in a few at a time.
1. I could let students choose some mini-research projects within the larger unit. 2. I could connect the main themes to their lives. 3. I could structure a debate about some of the key ideas.	Giving students some power and control might help boost their engagement. They will each choose one mini-topic to study.	**Class Discussion:** One week later, a class discussion revealed that students were enjoying the unit more and were more interested in the content.	I'll check in again in another week to see how things are going.
1. I will keep my main lesson to a maximum of 10 minutes. 2. We will do a movement activity right before the lesson starts.	I'm going to keep my lessons to no more than 10 minutes.	**Stopwatch:** After one week, I've kept four of five lessons timed to under 10 minutes. Students have been more focused, and I have had more time for one-on-one coaching.	I'll never go back! When I keep my lessons short, I've had to be more concise, and we've had more time for students to do work.

Ensure That Goal Setting Is Grounded in Student Needs But Focused on Your Actions

All of the examples outlined in the figures entail challenges involving our students, but the goals have to do with our own behavior. Consider what might happen if our goal is for all students to get a 100 percent on an upcoming math test. First, that goal may be unrealistic unless we create a test that is so easy that it does not really assess new learning. Second, we are on dangerous ground when our goal setting involves variables that we cannot control. Sure, it would be great if all of our students completely mastered the content on the math test, but we cannot control how well they study or how much sleep they get the night before the exam. We cannot control whether they are distracted by personal life events. So, it may be simply an unattainable dream to have all students ace a math test. Our goals should reflect *our* actions, not the actions of others.

Conclusion

It is no coincidence that in an age when teachers seem to be losing control of their voices in the classrooms and outside forces are assessing and setting unattainable or unrealistic goals for us, so many teachers are feeling disheartened and discouraged. Although we may not be able to single-handedly eliminate these pressures and demands, we can focus on the effectiveness of our own teaching. Gathering data based on our students' needs can help us set appropriate goals for our teaching to improve our practice and gain a sense of competence in the classroom.

There is great power here. When we know that we have some control over our teaching, when we know that we have the ability to achieve goals and improve our skills, we become more confident in our own competence. As we see our students responding positively to our efforts and see our skill level rising, we become more energetic and enthusiastic about teaching. Teaching itself is more enjoyable when we know we are successful teachers.

SPOTLIGHT ON A HEALTHY TEACHER

Evelyn, 5th Grade Teacher

Evelyn has been teaching 5th grade for 22 years. She is an energetic teacher with an engaging personality and a reputation for being firm but fair with her students. She often requests that the toughest students in the grade be placed with her, because she loves finding ways to connect with and help students who are struggling.

Clearly a master teacher, Evelyn presents a quiet confidence when you talk with her. She smiles proudly when showing off the work her students are doing and doesn't deflect compliments about her teaching. "Wow! These science projects are incredible!" she hears. "You must be doing a lot of great work to get your students to do such neat things." She replies, "Thanks! We've all been working hard in here." She pauses and adds, "Next year, I have an idea that will make this even better!"

Evelyn does several things to help her feel good about herself as a teacher. She keeps a daily journal about her teaching. Each page is divided into two columns: Successes and Next Steps. These categories allow her to focus on what is going well while also extending her thinking in a positive way to help herself get even better. Evelyn also focuses on attainable and measurable goals. "Right now," she explains, "my goal is to shorten the direct whole class instruction portion of my math lessons. I've noticed that I tend to talk too much when explaining a math concept, and half of my kids check out before the lesson is over. I timed my lessons for a week and discovered that I was talking for an average of 22 minutes to begin math class. My goal is to bring that down to 12. This week, I've been hanging right around 14, so I'm getting better! I've noticed that my students are more engaged during the lessons, and I'm still getting all of my teaching points in."

When asked how she does not let the daily distractions and stresses of teaching get her down, she shrugs. "Life's too short to worry about all of that little stuff," she says. "Focus on what you can do. Do it well. Let the rest go. It will all turn out okay."

CHAPTER 6

Fun: The Importance of Positive Engagement

Teaching should be fun. That's right—fun! This idea should not be revolutionary, but I worry that in today's age of schoolhouse pressure cookers and standardized curricula, it may sound that way. The daily act of teaching and the company of our students and colleagues should bring us pleasure. In fact, the need for fun is right up there with our needs for belonging and significance.

What do I mean when I use the word *fun*? A myriad of feelings and emotions are associated with fun, but when I think of the kind of fun we should enjoy at school, two forms come to mind: simple light-hearted pleasure and deep engagement. The first kind comes from the natural enjoyment of our students and the simple pleasures of being around other people. We might have a pleasant conversation with a colleague, enjoy the funny antics of a student, or have a comic scene unfold in the course of a class activity. This kind of fun is important, and it should not be dismissed as mere frivolity. I know there are still teachers out there who believe that teachers should not smile until December, but I would not want to be one. Would you?

The second kind of fun, deep engagement, comes when we become so engrossed in a task that we lose track of time or have the pleasurable sensation that athletes refer to as being "in the zone." The task itself might be something that we would not typically classify as fun (e.g., reading student essays, having a writing conference, or being in a heated philosophical discussion), but there is definite pleasure associated with losing oneself in a task. In this chapter, we will explore ways we can make sure that we are building opportunities for both lighthearted fun and deep engagement into our daily lives.

Why Fun Is So Important

Before we dive into *how* we can make sure we are having fun, let's discuss *why* it is so important. Just like belonging and significance, fun is a basic human emotional need. When we have fun, our spirits are high, we enjoy life, and we are more pleasant to be around. We are happier and healthier. Laughter has a number of positive health benefits, including boosting our immune systems, preventing heart disease, lowering stress hormones, and reducing pain (Smith, Kemp, & Segal, 2009). Quite simply, when we have fun, we are healthier.

When we are having fun, we can also let small annoyances roll off our backs more easily, and we have more positive energy for our students. Research has shown that teachers are more committed to their schools when they are positively engaged in work (Hakanen, Bakker, & Schaufeli, 2006). We're also more likely to deal well with the pressure and challenges that come with being a teacher. This revelation came to me as I was watching some pregame interviews before a Major League baseball playoff game. I noticed that the interviewers kept asking the same basic questions to the players, and each of the players gave some variation of the same answer. The interview, invariably, went something like this:

> **Reporter:** There's a lot of stress and pressure to do well in the playoffs. How do you plan to deal with that pressure so that you're prepared? What's your mind-set going into the game?

> **Player:** I'm just going to relax and have fun. This is what it's all about. We play the whole season to get to this point, so the best thing to do is enjoy the moment. If you get tense or try and push too hard, you're going to make mistakes. You've just got to have fun.

It's true. When we are having fun, we are loose and relaxed and more likely to think clearly and stay positive—just the kind of mind-set we need to survive in the pressure-cooker atmosphere of public school teaching today.

Increasing Our Sense of Fun

It is a cliché, I know, but life is simply too short to spend most of our time doing something we do not enjoy. The rest of this chapter describes how we can make being with students and working at school more fun.

Breathe Life into Curricula

So many of us are now saddled with prescriptive curricula that are supposed to be delivered in the same way, at the same time, and even with the same words, regardless of the culture of our students, the community in which they live, or their strengths and interests. Not only are these vapid, scripted curricula (which tend to lower standards, not raise them) deadly for our students, but they also rob our teaching of creativity and energy.

We can readily make our curricula more fun, not just for our students but for ourselves as well. We just need to be a little creative. Let me share an example from my own teaching. I mentioned earlier my frustration with the scripted math curriculum that our district had adopted. After a few years, I started to move away from using the math curriculum as my sole teaching tool and began to think of it more as a resource. I followed the general scope and sequence of the math book, using the activities that fit my students particularly well. Some games in the program were especially fun and useful. I then created my own lessons that fit the goals and guidelines of the curriculum that were more engaging—more hands-on with more differentiation and choice for students—and skipped lessons that were particularly bland or developmentally a bad fit for my students. We created a geometric quilt using the framework of the chapter on geometry that we proudly hung in our classroom. We did scavenger hunts around the classroom and the school for real-world uses of fractions and decimals. We played games to practice place value. Not only did the students enjoy math more, but so did I! The daily lessons were more fun for me because I knew that they matched my students' needs and that students would enjoy them. The planning itself was fun as I became deeply engaged in the creative process of crafting lessons and activities based on what was best for my students. Instead of feeling like the robotic conduit of the scripted math curriculum, I felt like a teacher again.

If you, like so many others, are struggling with dull curricula that seem disconnected from your students, you might want to liven things up a bit but are unsure of where to start. Here are some ways to help make what we teach more enjoyable:

• **Keep the good stuff, and make it the focus.** Begin by identifying the best parts of the curricula you have. Skim through that middle school reading anthology and look for the short stories that are most engaging for your students. Consider how you could use these stories as jumping-off places for units of study or even a series of lessons and class discussions. In my experience, even the worst curricula and programs out there still have something good to offer. Ironically, they often suggest really fun activities in the margins of the text or at the ends of chapters, and because of this placement, they rarely get used. For example, the end of a dry math lesson might present a game for kids who finish early or need an extension, and the game might better teach the skill than the lesson that precedes it. So, ditch the lesson and use the fun activity as the main vehicle for instruction! Comb through the lesson and make sure that the main point is being covered, or figure out how to weave it in. You and your students will have much more energy and fun.

• **Integrate, in a balanced way, your own interests and passions.** What do you *love* to do that you would enjoy sharing with students? Do you enjoy crafts? Do you like to build? Do you love to debate? Whatever it is, figure out how to weave your own interests and passions into your curricula. However, integrating our own interests comes with a caveat: we must make sure that we are blending our interests with the curricula in place, not replacing what we are supposed to be teaching with what we want to teach instead. For instance, I once saw a teacher who had a passion for sailing and lighthouses teach an entire unit on these topics that was not connected to the main curricula. Balance your personal interests with your teaching. Your passion for the work will fire up your creative juices, giving you great energy for planning and teaching that will get your students fired up and excited. Here are a few examples of how teachers have done this:

> A couple of years ago, I saw a presentation by the Massachusetts Teacher of the Year. He was a 3rd grade teacher who had a passion for making movies. He wove moviemaking into various aspects of the science and social studies curricula. His students used reading, writing, memorization, creative thinking skills, artwork, and many other skills as they wrote, acted, filmed, directed, designed sets, and produced great movies.

> A middle school teacher I know has a passion for hiking and camping. Part of her curriculum in science is a study of biology and ecosystems. She designed a three-day hiking and camping trip to the mountains with her class where students examined the geology, ecology, and biology of the region. At night she conducted astronomy lessons.

> A teacher who was required to teach a unit examining various elements of fiction had her class watch her favorite movie, *The Princess Bride*, as a springboard for the unit.

• **Use students' interests and passions.** One of the worst parts of scripted curricula is that they rarely pay any attention (how could they?) to the individual interests, talents, and strengths of our students. When our students' voices are absent from the teaching and learning in our classrooms, we can be pretty assured that no one is going to be having much fun. Whole books are devoted to differentiated instruction, multiple intelligence theory, academic choice, and other such topics. Let's consider a different perspective on *why* we should find ways of getting our students more invested in their learning. Most books and resources about these topics rightly argue that we should give students more power and control of their learning so that they will be more invested in their learning, thus deepening their academic engagement and helping them be better learners. Fair enough. (Having written a book about how to use independent research projects with elementary school students, I couldn't agree more.) However, there is another reason we should consider teaching like this: it's more fun for us, too! Consider the two scenarios presented in Figure 6.1. Which teacher is having more fun?

Figure 6.1	Comparing Two Classrooms

Lesson: In each of the following scenarios, an 8th grade teacher and class are analyzing character development in short stories. Each class uses the same reading anthology.

Classroom A	Classroom B
Students have all read the same short story (from the anthology) and are now filling out a worksheet (from the anthology) to show how the main character changed from the beginning to the end of the story. The teacher, Ms. A., is walking around the class helping students as they work.	Students have all read a short story (some chose one from the anthology, and some chose one from other collections of short stories in the classroom) and are now showing how the main character changed from the beginning to the end of the story. They can fill in a worksheet (from the anthology), write an essay, create a cartoon, or conduct a mock interview with the main character. The teacher, Ms. B., is walking around the classroom helping students as they work.
About half the class is working. Ms. A. walks from desk to desk, checking on students and helping when needed. She comes to John, who has a blank paper.

"John, why haven't you started yet?" John shrugs. He hates writing, and assignments like this have turned into a daily battle. "Well, come on," she urges. John rolls his eyes and picks up his pencil. Ms. A. stands by John to see him start, but she is distracted by a trio of girls in the back of the room, who are huddling together and giggling. As soon as she walks away, John puts his pencil back down.

"Girls! It's time to work!" she reminds them. They keep giggling until she begins walking to them, at which point they move back to their seats, sigh, and look at their blank papers.

Several students are dutifully working on their assignment, but they look tired and disconnected. As Ms. A. scans the work being done, she feels frustrated and tired. Deep down inside, she empathizes with her students. She doesn't really like the story in the anthology, either. | Ms. B. surveys the class as they work. There is considerable noise in the room, and she is tempted to ask the class to quiet down a bit, but she notices that nearly everyone is on task, and the noise is a result of excited chatter about their work.

John, a reluctant writer but avid artist, raises his hand. "Ms. B., I'm stuck. I want to draw a cartoon from the story I read, but I'm not sure where to start." Ms. B. coaches John to get him going, and soon he is eagerly drafting some sketches.

The girls in the back are getting a bit loud, so Ms. B. moves toward them. They are collaborating on an interview of the character from the story they all read, laughing as they try out different British accents.

Students around the room are engaged in their work. They eagerly share their work with Ms. B. and with each other. Ms. B. is able to offer advice and coach some students to help deepen their understanding of character development. Along the way, she hears about a couple of new stories that she has not read yet that she wants to check out herself. |

When we allow our students to have more control over their learning and use their own strengths and talents, they are more invested and engaged learners. And this is important: when our students are more invested and engaged, so are we. We have more energy for our students, we are more likely to be creative in our lesson designs, and the act of teaching is more pleasurable.

Be Playful and Creative with Curricula

Think creatively about other ways you can make daily assignments and projects more lively and fun. Some of the best learning activities I have encountered, both as a teacher and as a student, were simply novel yet fun ways to connect students to the curricula. Here are just a few:

A high school physics teacher came up with a unique way to assess his students' understanding of some of the basic laws of physics. Students watched a couple of Roadrunner and Coyote cartoons and had to determine which laws of physics were being broken through the course of the shows.

A 3rd grade teacher was teaching a unit on letter writing. She had students form pen pals with seniors at a local nursing home. Students hand-delivered the letters each week (they were able to walk to the senior center from the school). They read their letters to their pen pals and then stayed for some informal visiting time.

A middle school teacher was studying astronomy with her class and heard that the space shuttle would be visible from their town. She invited any students who could make it to join her on the soccer field at 5:00 a.m. when the shuttle would be visible. Two-thirds of the class showed up! They saw the shuttle and then went inside to have hot chocolate and watch a fun science video about outer space before school started.

A high school English teacher was working on a creative writing unit with his sophomores. He contacted a nearby elementary school to see whether a class would be up for a project. His sophomores spent time interviewing the 4th graders to learn their names, interests, favorite foods and sports teams, and so on, and then returned to class to write short stories that used the 4th graders as main characters and incorporated as much of the information they had gathered from their interviews into their stories as they could. When finished, the high school students returned to the 4th grade class to share their final stories.

Each of these stories illustrates how a little creativity on the teachers' part made some exciting learning opportunities available for their students. Chances are these activities will be remembered by both students and teachers for years to come. And let's not forget the focus of this chapter: they were all fun! Students were engaged. Teachers were engaged. The daily act of teaching is more pleasurable when these kinds of learning activities are happening.

Carve Out Time for Deep Engagement

All right, I can just see some eyes rolling out there. You may be thinking, "Well, yeah, I'd love to teach like that more often, but I just don't have time for it! We've got meetings before and after school that take away my planning time, and we're all so crunched for class time that I just don't see how this is possible." I hear you. It's important to recognize that this kind of teaching does take time. It's easier and requires less time to simply deliver the lesson straight out of the math program than to come up with a more creative and fun way to teach the same content. In the next chapter, we will explore some strategies for how to balance our time effectively so that we are spending our time on things that will pay greater dividends. For now, simply remember that deep engagement leads to greater student involvement and thus heightened learning—and fun, to boot. Dedicating time to this effort is always time well spent.

Do Not Assume You Can't Play

I was conducting a workshop recently on how to structure independent research with elementary students. Teachers were interested in and excited about the idea of blending their literacy teaching with science and social studies content through research projects. As the day progressed, however, several teachers started to voice concerns. They were worried about deviating from the reading anthology they were working on.

Two distinct mind-sets were apparent among many of the teachers at this school. Some people were convinced that their principal and assistant principal were watching them like hawks and would immediately pounce if they strayed from the prescribed curricula. Other teachers had the reverse assumption. They believed that their administrators would be supportive of them if they decided to try something new.

The teachers who assumed their administrators would not support more creative and innovative teaching were really missing out. I talked with the assistant principal and discovered that she absolutely supported teachers taking risks and trying out new teaching strategies. These teachers had been holding themselves back unnecessarily and feeling resentful about it. Do not make the same mistake: inject fun into your teaching, for your students' benefit and your own.

Create a Fun and Engaging Classroom Environment

In the chapter about taking care of our most basic needs, we looked at how important it is to create a pleasant, welcoming classroom environment. We might get a minifridge so we can have some healthy foods and cold water on hand. We can paint a wall to make the colors more pleasing or add some plants or a water fountain to help us connect with the natural world. Now let's consider how we can add elements to our classrooms that will make them more fun and engaging.

• **Incorporate personal interests and passions (again!).** Just as we can integrate some of our own interests into our curricula, we can do the same thing for our classroom spaces. Here's a way to share your love of lighthouses and sailing, for example, without devoting extra teaching time to the subject. Add a couple of lighthouse models to a shelf in the back of the room, or put up a calendar with lighthouses on the wall near the door. Whether you love lighthouses, dogs, college football, or painting, find ways to incorporate these interests into your classroom in small and subtle ways. We spend a large percentage of our waking lives in our classrooms, so giving ourselves a few reminders of our lives outside school can only make being in these spaces more enjoyable.

Chances are the artifacts in the room will also spark conversations with your students and help you make positive connections with them. I once met a teacher who was a huge fan of Superman (and at 6'2" tall, he probably looked the part to his 3rd grade students). He was constantly whistling the theme song from the movie while he worked and making quirky Superman references throughout the day. He even had a cape hung up in his classroom. Quite simply, he had fun all day, and you know his students did as well! Figure 6.2 shares some other examples of teachers bringing their interests and passions into their classrooms.

Figure 6.2	Incorporating Teachers' Interests in the Classroom
Marine biology	A middle school teacher was fascinated with marine life. (He didn't teach biology, though.) He set up a saltwater aquarium in his classroom filled with animal life that he netted himself in Long Island Sound. The tank was a constant source of entertainment for the teacher and his students.
Gardening	A teacher started new plants from cuttings on the back window sill. Hanging tomato plants were suspended from the ceiling.
Reptiles	I've always been fascinated by snakes and lizards, so I often kept them in tanks in my classroom. Students helped care for them and often stayed inside for recess to hold them.
Music	One teacher's love of music resulted in quotes from favorite composers over the doorway to the class and quiet, soothing music being played at various times of the day.
National parks	A 1st grade teacher had been to nearly all of the national parks. She had pine cones and tassels out for students to see, posters of the national parks, and pictures of herself hiking in various parts of the room.
Garfield	A colleague of mine absolutely loved the cartoon cat Garfield. She had a Garfield calendar. She sipped coffee from Garfield mugs. She had a couple of posters of Garfield on the walls. Students always had great ideas for teacher presents around the holidays!

• **Seize opportunities for collateral learning.** As just mentioned, we will often make interesting personal connections with students, which can reinforce our (and their) sense of belonging in the classroom. Valuable teaching and learning opportunities will also pop up at unexpected times. For example, while standing in line, a student sees a picture of you whitewater rafting and says, "Where were you rafting?" You quickly point to a map of the United States to show the Animas River in Durango, Colorado. Another example might happen around the fish tank. A student happens to look over and see a sea star prying open a mussel shell, and everyone takes a five-minute break from work to check it out. A friend and colleague of mine, Andy Dousis, refers to these as "collateral learning" moments. They are not planned or part of the normal curricula. But they can often spark great conversations or help students develop new interests that can be very important. And oh, yeah—they are also really fun!

   • **Balance your personal interests with your students' needs.** Just as when we bring our own passions and interests into the curricula, we need to make sure not to overdo it when adding some personal touches to our classrooms. A couple of pictures of our hobby in the back corner of the room can be a nice personal touch. If we devote a whole wall of our classroom to that hobby, however, we may be neglecting the content of the classroom. One or two pictures of our children on our desk or on a shelf may be a nice way to think of our families throughout the day. A collection of personal photos and mementos from family plastered all around our desk gives the impression that we are not present with our students. When we overdo the personal touches of our lives in our classrooms, we may be conveying the idea that we should be the center of attention in the room instead of our students and their learning.

Enjoy the People with Whom We Work

Another important way we can have fun while we work is to make sure to enjoy the people around us. We are surrounded by students and colleagues all day long, so let's make sure those interactions are enjoyable.

Enjoy Your Students

   I was once talking with a couple whose son was struggling through his first year of teaching middle school. Their son was having a difficult time maintaining control with the students in the class, and they asked me for advice that they could pass on to him about classroom management. Before I could start to offer advice about effective classroom management for a middle school science class, I asked, "What are his favorite qualities of young adolescents? What does he really love about middle school kids?" They raised their eyebrows in surprise, looked at each other a bit uncomfortably, and replied, "You know, we're not sure he really likes adolescents." I was then able to give some advice: "Tell him to find a different job."

It will be awfully hard for us to really enjoy our work if we do not enjoy the characteristics of the students with whom we work. Kindergarten teachers need to enjoy students who are concrete and literal. Sixth grade teachers need to see humor in students' propensity to argue and test limits, and they need to understand that these behaviors are normal for 11-year-olds.

A good friend of mine taught 3rd grade for quite a few years and enjoyed it, but she didn't *love* it. She felt like she needed a change, so she took a few classes and became certified as a high school English teacher. This is where she found her true calling. Now she *loves* the daily interactions with her students. She enjoys high schoolers' dry and quick wits. She loves engaging them in debates. She enjoys the challenge of working through difficult concepts in literature with them. When I discuss teaching with her, her voice rings with a new energy.

As fundamental as it may be to enjoy the company of our students, it's also important to recognize that doing so can be really difficult at times. Tight schedules, testing pressures, and challenging student behaviors can all make us tense and hard-pressed to appreciate and enjoy our students. The following suggestions offer some possibilities for finding daily pleasure in our interactions with students.

• **Find a good fit.** Like the friend I just described, make sure you are teaching an age that you truly enjoy. If you love teaching but do not love the age you teach, find a new position that will be a better match for you.

• **Brush up on child development.** When was the last time you refreshed your knowledge of the developmental ages and stages of the students with whom you work? Knowing that it's natural for 14-year-olds to be rambunctious and loud or that 9-year-olds can be anxious and nervous can allow you to smile when it happens, knowing that they are supposed to be like that.

• **Shift your mind-set.** Often, little misbehaviors of students can build up until we are really frustrated. Remember, kids are trying to get their needs met. Their misbehaviors are more about them than us. When we remember to disconnect ourselves from students' misbehaviors, we can keep our energy levels higher and appreciate all of our students more easily.

• **Take time to observe.** Instead of hurrying through every moment of the day, take a minute or two to observe your students. Watch them as they work with each other, and find time to enjoy their interactions.

• **Give students your full attention.** Sometimes we miss great chances to have pleasurable conversations and interactions with our students because we are multitasking. A student enters the room and tries to tell us about her weekend, and we half listen as we shuffle papers, check e-mail, or straighten a table. Instead, we should make full eye contact with that student and enjoy that she wants to share a bit of her life with us.

• **Be playful.** Crack jokes. Tell ridiculous stories. Use comic strips to make a teaching point. Make silly analogies. Be a little gross ("Jimmy ate 345 slugs for breakfast and another 567 for lunch. How many slugs did he eat all together?"). There's nothing like a lively sense of humor to keep everyone in a better mood! I think the only thing I remember from high school chemistry is Mr. Sweetser's favorite pun, dead-panned: "Max Planck was bored [board] with his name."

Enjoy Your Colleagues

I was recently working with a group of elementary school teachers in Virginia. As one of them came to our meeting at lunchtime, I saw she had a small stack of papers and was furiously tabulating some sort of data, trying to finish it up before our small-group work began for the afternoon. "Carmela, what are you working on?" I asked. She chuckled and said, "Our fantasy happy hour scores." I replied, "Your *what*?" She laughed again and went on to explain. Apparently, she and some colleagues were in a fantasy football league at school, and someone complained that she didn't really know enough about football to play well. She wanted something she could be good at, so someone invented the idea of a happy hour fantasy league. They came up with a scoring system to award points at happy hours. For example, you get five points simply for showing up but are awarded a bonus of two points if you are the first one to arrive. You lose three points if you leave first, though. You get one point if the bartender knows your name and two points if you get carded. You lose two points if you are the first to go to the bathroom or if you spill a drink or drop food. And you earn a whopping five points for being the last to leave. Not only did these teachers invent this elaborate scoring system, but they went to a happy hour and really kept score! As a bonus activity, one of the teachers records silly and ridiculous quotes from the night for posterity. Their goal is to go once a month. I asked Carmela to write this activity up for me and send me an e-mail, and she ended her note with the following reflection: "We had a really great time at the happy hour. It was a great time to relax and just be normal people with our colleagues."

It is no coincidence that this school in Virginia is one of my favorites to visit and work with. Teachers there enjoy one another's company but are also serious and willing to question and challenge one another while staying professional and collegial. Teachers like these can combat stress through using humor to support each other (see Mawhinney, 2008).

Of course, I would not recommend that every school develop a fantasy happy hour committee, but we can work at enjoying our colleagues in many other ways. Consider a few more ideas:

• **Join positive colleagues for committee work.** Wouldn't you rather be on a social studies curriculum committee with a bunch of fun and passionate educators than a party planning committee with a bunch of sour curmudgeons? Seek out colleagues who smile a lot, talk enthusiastically about students, and have lots of positive energy.

• **Plan lunch dates.** Make sure you have a regular time to connect with fun colleagues for lunch (or breakfast or a midmorning snack break). Share a joke and a laugh.

• **Work together.** Sometimes paperwork is simply a little more enjoyable with some company. It is sort of like parallel play for teachers. You are grading science exams. Your colleague is planning a social studies unit. You do not talk (much). Time passes more quickly when someone else is in the room. Good food helps, too!

• **Be playful.** Joke around and be playful with a colleague next door. You will feel lighter, and your students will learn valuable lessons (while laughing right along with you!)

• **Avoid negative colleagues.** As much as possible, do not spend time with colleagues who are constantly griping and complaining. Their negative energy will suck out your own healthy attitude.

The Power of Rewarding Professional Development

I was talking with a kindergarten teacher recently. The previous Friday she had taken a professional day to help craft a new assessment tool for her district. She hunkered down in her living room with her computer and got an incredible amount of work done. At the end of the day, she was totally fired up. "That was so much fun! I got so immersed in the work that the day flew by!" she exclaimed. She also let me know that on Monday morning she was still flying high from her productive day on Friday, and she could not wait to get back to school.

To make professional development especially engaging and enjoyable, consider a few factors:

• **How do you learn best?** Do you prefer solitary activities like reading, watching videos, or journaling, or do you learn best by engaging in conversation and debate?

• **Where are you likely to be most productive and comfortable?** Is the teachers' room or the library a place where you can get lots of work done, is home a better place to work, or do you prefer totally off-site PD like attending a workshop or a graduate class?

• **When are you most productive and energetic?** What time of day do you feel at your best? If you can engage in PD on your own schedule, you can carve out times that work best for you.

Conclusion

Teaching will not always be fun. There are days when the best we can do is duck our heads, set our teeth, and get through. However, these days should not become the norm. We should generally enjoy our work and look forward to going to school. Like just about everything else we have been exploring in this book, it is our responsibility to make sure that we are taking care of this need. If we are struggling with enjoying our work on a daily basis, then it is up to us to figure out how to feel a greater sense of fun and positive engagement at school. Remember, it's not being selfish to take care of ourselves. Taking care of our own most basic needs is one of our responsibilities to our students. When we are having fun, our students will, too!

SPOTLIGHT ON A HEALTHY TEACHER

Mark, High School History Teacher

"You just got to love this class," Mark says with a wry smile and a shake of his head. "They just get so *into* their work!" Mark's class of freshmen are preparing the final points of a class debate on comparing and contrasting the Vietnam War and the wars in Iraq and Afghanistan. Noticing a group of students getting pretty animated at the back of the room, he quickly moves over there to see how they are doing. While working with his students, Mark is fully engaged. He kneels down to make good eye contact and asks piercing questions, clearly interested in what they have to say. His love of history is apparent, and so is his love of working with adolescents. "Kids this age are so alive!" he gushes. "Once they trust you and they know it's really safe to say what they think, you can have such cool class discussions!"

Mark is also quick to point out that he does not love every part of his job. Staff meetings, curriculum development committees, and fund-raisers are three things he says he cannot stand. So, he tries to focus his time and energy on activities he loves: working with students and trying out new lessons and projects. He spends an hour every Saturday morning reading education blogs and magazines, looking for new ideas to try out. He also coaches the school's debate team and works as a student advisor, where he gets to work more closely with individual kids and small groups.

Talking with Mark's students reveals their impressions of him as a teacher. "Mr. Safford is cool," remarks one. "He really gets into stuff. You kinda have to get into it, too, you know?" Another student nods. "Mr. S. is one of those teachers everyone in the school hopes they get. It's not that he's easy. He's not. But he makes you think, and he really cares."

When Mark hears about these comments, he smiles and asks, "How could you not love this job?"

CHAPTER 7

Balance: The Importance of Planning Our Time and Energy

Chances are, while reading this book, you have been thinking about areas of your life and aspects of your teaching that might need more or different attention. A vague but powerful urge to "get more balanced" is likely percolating in your gut. But then you look at the stack of papers waiting for you on the kitchen counter and peek at your schedule for next week (which includes two IEP meetings during your planning periods, three committee meetings after school, and a classroom play that must be ready by Friday—and that's just what's going on at school!), and you think, "Okay, I'll get balanced in a couple of weeks."

Before we get too far into exploring ways to better balance our work and school lives, we need to acknowledge a simple truth and even a battle cry of teachers everywhere: "We don't have enough time." Really—we don't. Do any of these common statements sound familiar?

• "Every year, more and more gets piled on our plates, and nothing is ever taken away."

• "We just don't have enough time to do everything we're supposed to do!"

• "I try as hard as I can, but I just can't keep up with the workload."

Remember the personal research I conducted about 10 years ago in my classroom, when I concluded that you just cannot teach 5 hours and 5 minutes of content in 3 hours and 40 minutes? This is just one small illustration of the time crunch that most teachers experience.

Teachers all over the country are struggling with an unreasonable workload. A recent threat by the Palm Beach County teachers' union is an example of how overworked we all know teachers are. After a series of changes to their scheduling that was requiring yet more demands on their already pinched time, the teachers' union threatened to work only its bare minimum contract hours (Green, 2009). What's telling (and amusing, if you think about it) is that the threat itself makes it clear that we really do not have the time we need. Consider this: the teachers were not threatening to strike but simply threatening to work only as much as they are technically supposed to! This threat shows that it's common knowledge that we do not have enough time, because if we were to work only our contract hours, students' education would be significantly diminished.

Handling the Time Crunch

First, we can stop trying to do it all. If we do not have time to teach everything we are supposed to, and if we really do not have enough time to be on all of those committees and coach the debate team and plan an integrated unit with three other colleagues, then we should stop trying to. That does not mean that we just cash in our chips and quit the profession or, worse, do the bare minimum and sip coffee in the teachers' lounge, waiting patiently for retirement. Instead, consider the following suggestions for focusing our time and energy to help us become more productive and positive.

Carve Out Time for Nonnegotiables

Sally Kitts, a teacher and educational consultant from North Carolina, loves to tell a story to teachers about a philosophy professor who stands before his class with an empty jar. He fills the jar with rocks and asks the class, "Is the jar full?" The class acknowledges that it is. The professor then pulls out a sack of pebbles and pours the pebbles into the jar. The pebbles fill in the gaps between the rocks. The professor again asks, "Is the jar full?" The class nods and says that yes, *now* the jar is full. The professor then pulls out a sack of sand and pours it into the jar. The sand fills in the remaining gaps between the rocks and pebbles. The professor then asks the class, "What would happen if I started with the sand? There wouldn't have been any room for the pebbles or rocks. In life, the rocks are the most important things—family, friends, good health. The pebbles are the second-most important things—your work, your house, your car. Everything else in life is just sand. Be careful not to fill up your life with the sand, or you will find there isn't room for the rocks and pebbles!"

One of the reasons it can be so hard for us to maintain some semblance of balance in our lives as teachers is that we have not carved out time for things that should take priority over others. Consider writing a list of the things that are most important in life. What might that list include? Family dinners, weekend hikes with friends, knitting on the couch with a fluffy dog, and dancing might be on one teacher's list, whereas another might list traveling with her sister, wildlife photography, Saturday morning breakfasts with her parents, and playing the piano.

Now consider your nonnegotiables at school. What roles and responsibilities are most important? Of course, there's daily class time with students. We also need sufficient planning time. What else is on your list? Team meetings? Committee work? Parent communication? There are certainly many possibilities. Decide which of these are truly on your list of nonnegotiables.

Figure Out What to Eliminate

List your current roles and responsibilities in and out of school. Some items from your nonnegotiable list are clearly not ones to eliminate. You may be required to have team meetings with colleagues every Wednesday morning. You may need to pick your daughter up from hockey practice each night. However, if you are truly swamped with committee work or other commitments that are getting in the way of you taking care of yourself, your family, or your students, figure out which ones you can drop. I recently talked with a middle school teacher who was drowning at work. He was on four committees that met regularly, he was a coach on the school's cross-country running team, and he has two young daughters at home. As the cross-country season came to a close (right around report card and conference time, of course), he hit a breaking point and decided to get off two committees and give his notice that he would not be coaching next year.

As you look at your schedule and lists of responsibilities, remember to consider which ones are helping you meet your needs for belonging, significance, positive engagement, and competence. We want to focus our involvement on these sorts of activities.

Learn to Say No

In researching this book, I often asked teachers for the qualities they would expect to see in healthy, balanced teachers. "They know how to say no" was the most common reply. If your plate is already full and someone invites you to join a new committee or an administrator asks you to take on another responsibility, it may be the most respectful thing you can do, for them as well as for you, to politely decline. If an administrator insists, ask her to help you figure out what current responsibility you should drop so you can take on the new one.

Saying no can be tough, but a mind-set shift will help. Often, when we accept a responsibility when we know we should decline, we worry that we are going to hurt someone's feelings or somehow disappoint someone. We do not want people to think that we don't want to help or are unwilling to pitch in. We *must* remind ourselves that we have to take care of ourselves in order to take care of others. If we take on too much, not only will we not have the time necessary to take on these new responsibilities, but we will be more tired and more stressed out with everything we do. As counterintuitive as it may seem, saying no may be more respectful and helpful in the long run to those whom we turn down.

Work More Efficiently

When we are working, we want to make sure to spend our time as well as possible. The more efficient we are when working, the more we will accomplish, which will help us give ourselves permission to not work quite so long. Here are some tips to consider:

• **Capitalize on your optimal time of day.** When are you most productive? If you are a morning person, consider setting aside time in the morning for your toughest work (e.g., planning and assessing) and saving lighter work (cleaning, organizing, etc.) for later in the day. If you work best in the evening, you may have more energy for tough school work after dinner. If so, consider exercising earlier in the day so that your evenings are free for school work.

• **Balance assignments.** Make sure you are not overwhelming yourself with the kinds of assignments and class projects you are taking on. When teaching 5th grade, I tried to have a unit that required a lot more planning and energy coincide with a unit that was easy for me to teach. A high school English teacher might make sure not to assign four different classes papers all due on the same day. Instead, a couple of classes might have papers due while others are in the middle of a project or completing an assignment that is easier to assess.

• **Look for a mismatch between your time and your goals.** Remember my mind-set shift around homework in Chapter 5? When I realized that homework was not worth tons of my time and energy, I was able to let it slip back into its proper place in my teaching life. Homework just wasn't at the top of my priority list. Do you have any practices that you may spend too much time on? Figure out how to minimize elements of your school day that do not have to do with important work for you and your students.

• **Minimize interruptions.** There's nothing like the blaring call of the intercom to stop the flow of a lesson or a planning session. Although we cannot eliminate all interruptions, we can try to minimize them:

　○ Intercom: Can you turn yours off? If so, keep it on only when needed. If not, ask the office to interrupt only with emergencies during certain hours.

　○ E-mail: Turn it off when you are working on the computer. Check it when you need to, but do not let instant notifications of incoming mail distract your writing or planning.

○ Drop-bys: When you need some uninterrupted time in your room, post a sign on the door: "Working Time: If possible, see me later." If this tactic does not work, try moving to a quiet location when planning.

○ Phone: Turn your phone off when you need some uninterrupted time.

Leverage the Strictness of a Schedule

I used to feel confined and restricted by the tight schedule I had to keep as a teacher. I had to be at school by 7:00 every day if I was going to have time to plan. I had to pick students up from lunch at 12:24. I had from 10:15 to 11:00 to plan each day.

Our rigid schedules can seem a bit stifling at times, but that strict structure is also highly beneficial in highlighting specific openings for our nonnegotiable roles and responsibilities. For example, we can plan a consistent exercise plan and carve out specific times to set aside for family and friends. Once we establish these habits and routines, sticking to them becomes automatic and does not require any more willpower than brushing our teeth each night. People with loose schedules can often struggle with knowing how to create healthy habits. They put off exercise knowing they can do it later. They are wedded to their BlackBerry® smartphones, always checking work e-mail and taking phone calls when they should be spending time with their families. With a sound schedule in hand, we can be proactive about planning our time. Like high school athletes whose grades are often higher during the sports season because they have to be better about planning their time, we can leverage our strict schedules to our advantage.

Try creating a schedule for a typical week. Include all activities and responsibilities that should be there, including your nonnegotiables, sleep, exercise, mealtimes, and family/friends time. The process of actually creating a schedule that forces you to consider all you do might have you scurrying to adjust some commitments. Once you have your schedule set, force yourself to stick with it for a few weeks—long enough to see how the rhythm of it feels. If you need to, adjust to make things work better. Consider the sample schedules in Figures 7.1 and 7.2.

Figure 7.1   Sarah's Schedule

Sara is a middle school teacher who teaches social studies and literacy. She is 25 and single.

	Monday	Tuesday	Wednesday	Thursday	Friday	Saturday	Sunday
6:00–7:30	Get up, get ready, breakfast, drive to school					Time for friends and leisure: hiking, biking, artwork, reading, etc.	Church and family time
7:30–10:00	With students, homeroom and social studies						
10:00–10:45	Planning period						
10:45–12:15	With students, literacy block						
12:15–1:00	Lunch with colleagues for social time						
1:00–2:00	With students, social studies, literacy						
2:00–3:30	*Field hockey	Team meeting	Field hockey	Staff meeting	†Field hockey		
3:30–5:00	District social studies committee	Planning and other school work (at school)					Planning
5:00–6:30	Drive home, relax, have dinner, fix lunch for next day						Fix snacks for the week
6:30–10:00	†Read, visit with friends, watch TV, other						
10:00–6:00	Sleep						

* During field hockey practice, Sarah runs with her team, getting in her exercise for the day.

† During field hockey season, Sarah has a game most Friday nights.

Figure 7.2   John's Schedule

John is a 3rd grade teacher. He is 45 and the father of four.

	Monday	Tuesday	Wednesday	Thursday	Friday	Saturday	Sunday
5:00–6:00	Exercise, running, sit-ups, push-ups					Family and self time	
6:00–7:30	Breakfast with family, help get kids ready for the day						
7:30–8:30	Grade-level meeting	Drive to school, listen to audio books					Community volunteer work with family
8:30–12:00	With students						
12:00–12:30	Lunch, planning time						
12:30–1:30	With students						
1:30–2:15	Planning period						Family time
2:15–3:30	With students						
3:30–5:00	Staff meeting						
5:00–8:00	Family time, including dinner						
8:00–9:00	Planning						Planning
9:00–5:00	Sleep						Sleep

The Blessing and Curse of Work Flexibility

Although we often have tight schedules during official school hours, in the last decade, the lines between school and home have blurred significantly. Laptops and cell phones that deliver e-mail make it possible for us to work just about anywhere. Many teachers have keys and passwords to security systems at their schools so that they can access buildings on the weekends and during vacations. On the one hand, this flexibility with work can allow us to work in ways that the previous generation of teachers never could have imagined. We can create elaborate multimedia projects while sitting on our couch at home. We can scan Web sites for students to use while sitting at our kid's soccer game. We can read and answer e-mails while hanging out with friends on the weekend. This technology-induced flexibility can be a great boon, allowing us to be more productive and connected to our teaching. On the other hand, it can also prevent us from disconnecting at all, making us feel like we are never really away from work or making it difficult to fully engage with friends and family. Here are some suggestions for how to insert some boundaries while still being connected:

• **Check e-mail selectively**. Give yourself a set time or two each day or on the weekend when you check and respond to e-mails. When it is not one of those times, do not even look at it.

• **Ignore phone calls.** If it is not a good time to talk, do not answer the phone. In fact, turn it off. You can always call someone back later. I used to tell parents, "Here's my home phone number. Call me whenever you have a question or concern. If it's not a good time for me to talk, I won't pick it up. But don't worry—leave me a message, and I'll get back to you."

• **Restrict your use of a laptop.** If you have a laptop you use for schoolwork, consider setting aside certain blocks of time when you will work. Then, when you are not working, turn it off, close it up, and put it out of the way. Leaving a laptop in a living room or in the kitchen is an invitation to "do just one little thing," which can then turn into several tasks gobbling an hour or two. If you have a laptop only for work, consider leaving it at school when you do not plan on working at home.

A Note to Perfectionists: Relax a Little

For those of us with perfectionist tendencies (a seemingly disproportionate number of teachers are afflicted with this condition), we might just need to relax a bit. Do you remember Cathy, my colleague who felt like her best would never be good enough? One year she was at school for days in July still putting the finishing touches on 1st grade take-home portfolios to send to families. They needed to be "just right." I tried to explain to her that parents would be happy with a collection of artifacts from their child's year and would not miss the decorative covers and extra work samples she was putting together. As a parent of schoolchildren myself, I am amazed at how little I really understand about what my children's teachers are doing. I see work that Ethan and Carly bring home, I visit their classrooms whenever possible, and I chat with them all the time about what they are doing in school, but I have absolutely no idea what kind of time and effort their teachers are spending or whether each project is great or simply good.

In our profession, Cathy is not an anomaly. Many teachers find themselves crippled with a workload that is somewhat self-imposed as they try to do things "just right." I certainly do not want to give the impression that we should coast through our work, settling for mediocrity. To the contrary, I believe it is vitally important for us to work hard to create a rich and stimulating educational experience for our students. At the same time, though, sometimes we need to be okay with doing "just" good work so that we do not deplete our energy reserves or frazzle our own nerves so that we cannot stay happy and healthy. In the end, it's better to create learning experiences for our students that can be realistically achieved within our healthy lifestyles than to stretch ourselves beyond reason to achieve perfection (which of course is unattainable anyway) and end up physically and emotionally worn out.

Ignore Your Schedule Every Now and Then

As much as we plan and set ourselves up for healthy routines and habits, there will be a few times during the year when we have to expect that we will be overwhelmed with school responsibilities. At the end of a semester, with exams to review, papers to grade, new units to plan, and IEP meetings to attend, we will likely need to put in some extra hours. Give yourself permission for some late nights and some weekends on the computer. However, as long as we have healthy habits to resume, we can survive these brief periods of craziness, knowing there is a light at the end of the tunnel.

This advice is sort of like allowing yourself to overeat on Thanksgiving, knowing that the day after, you'll be back to your normal healthy eating and exercise routines. After all, we cannot be healthy and balanced *all* of the time, can we? As a friend of mine likes to say, "Everything in moderation—even moderation!"

Balance doesn't just happen. We need to be thoughtful about how we structure our time. We need to make conscious decisions about what we do and when we do it. When we learn to balance our home and work responsibilities, carve out time for important work and weed out things that are lower priorities, and balance our intense work with much needed down time, we give ourselves a chance to lead a more sane and balanced life. We'll stay happier and healthier in general, and our students will be the ultimate beneficiaries!

SPOTLIGHT ON A HEALTHY TEACHER

Trisha, Middle School Math Teacher

Although she feels balanced now, Trisha says that she didn't always feel that way. "When I first started teaching," she recalls, "I spent just about every weekend at school. I was so disorganized, and I was at the steep end of the learning curve in just about every way. I had five different math classes, and each class had a huge variety of learning styles and challenges. I was trying to meet everyone where they were, but I hadn't even learned the curriculum yet. Plus, I had a real struggle with classroom management. Kids walked all over me my first couple of years. I almost quit."

When asked what the turning point was, she explains that there were a few. First, she took a workshop on effective classroom management, specifically designed for middle school teachers. Once she had the skills she needed to keep her classes running smoothly, she was able to focus on her curricula. She also carved out time to meet with colleagues who shared strategies for creating groups within her classes to receive some targeted skill work.

"I was still spending too much time at school, though," she admits. "I developed some pretty bad habits my first few years. I was really inefficient about planning—always skipping from one thing to another before I finished anything. I also let papers stack up and got really behind with assessing daily work."

The major turning point was getting married and starting a family. Once other people outside school needed her time and attention, Trisha had to rein in some things. She started assigning work that was easier to assess and gave herself permission to check daily work without correcting and marking every paper. Today she also has experience to fall back on, so when time is getting really crunched, she has some good projects and activities to present that do not require too much planning. She has even made time to exercise four days a week, and she takes an organic cooking class every Saturday morning.

So how did she achieve this balance? She says that it was very deliberate. "I made a list," she says. "I listed all of the things I thought I had to do and then decided which ones were most important and which ones I could let go." She also worked out a schedule with her husband so that she knows which mornings she can exercise and which mornings she needs to be home. "There are still times when I get overwhelmed, especially when report cards are due. But I know it won't last long. I've got some good routines that keep me in line!"

Afterword

Have you ever noticed that once you start working on something that captures your attention, it can be hard to put it down? I sure have. Years ago, I built a rock wall as part of the entryway to the first house that Heather and I bought together. It was a simple structure, just stacked rock—no mortar—that acted as a retaining wall for a small hill. It was sort of like putting a big jigsaw puzzle together. I worked at layering the rock so that the top stayed level while also varying the thickness of stones in a particular area to give it a somewhat organic feel. This project took me a couple weeks to complete because I was working on it mostly before school early in the morning, and because I disassembled it at one point when I was not happy with how it was coming out. During those two weeks (and actually for quite a while afterward), I felt like all I could see everywhere I went were rock walls. Every neighborhood I drove through seemed filled with them. I started noticing walls that I had driven by for years without a second glance. I found myself sketching them while doodling in idle moments. The cinder block walls in my classroom took on a new look. I even caught myself scanning the edge of the road as I drove places, looking for nice flat rocks with good color. To Heather's great embarrassment, I actually stopped the car a few times and quickly commandeered stones from the edges of highway construction projects.

When I was finished with the wall, I was quite pleased with how it looked. It was level across the top, had a nice curve, and included a variety of colors and textures, while still coming together as a cohesive whole. The small flower garden that I planted just behind the wall softened some rough spots and really made our entryway pop.

However, I found it hard to stop. I kept readjusting the top layer of rocks, trying to perfect the combination or layering a little more dirt under a particular stone so it was angled just right. I had to fight the urge not to take the whole thing apart (again) to fix one spot in the middle that was a bit crooked. I still scanned the sides of the road for nice rocks.

A similar mentality challenged me in writing this book. Although I have spent a considerable amount of time over the past few years reading, thinking, and writing about how to stay healthy and balanced as a teacher, I feel as though I could keep on going forever. I wrote the first draft of this book several years ago and spent a lot of time tinkering, adjusting, reading portions to friends and colleagues, and tinkering some more. After receiving some suggestions for improvements from ASCD, I basically rewrote the entire book, adding new research, deleting whole chapters, and adding new ones. Just after I sent my revised draft into ASCD, PBS aired "This Emotional Life," hosted by social psychologist Daniel Gilbert. I found myself mentally adding new ideas and even new chapters to this book as I watched. Then I heard an interview on NPR one morning with Daniel Pink about his new book, *Drive*, and immediately bought the book. His research about the importance of autonomy in the workplace as it relates to creativity and motivation is fantastic, and I wanted to spend another six months reading and thinking about the ideas he presents. Every time I talk with a teacher, every time I read an educational blog or news article, new ideas and new questions present themselves. At some point, however, as with any project, it's time to take a deep breath, step back, and give yourself permission to let it go (at least for a while).

So, I'd like to give a couple of last reminders and make a request before we finish for now. First the reminders:

• **Take small steps.** When tackling a life change such as exercising more, eating better, or rearranging your schedule, it can be tempting to take on too much all at once. Inevitably, taking on too much means almost certain failure. Instead of cutting out all sweets from your diet, just get the candy dish off your desk. Instead of trying to work out an hour a day, start with walking for 15 minutes four days a week. Instead of ditching your whole prescriptive writing program, try crafting one new unit that uses the writing program as a framework but embeds some more student choice. A few small steps will likely result in success, which will fuel your fire to try more small steps.

• **Start now.** It might be tempting at this point to say, "Okay, I've got some ideas for getting healthier, but I'll start them when X happens. X could be any number of factors, such as "when my spouse changes her schedule" or "when my course load eases up a bit" or "when the next school year begins" or "when my children are just a little bit older." There will always be an X factor that stands as an excuse not to start building healthier habits. One X factor will lead to the next, and nothing will ever change. Think of one change you could make tomorrow, write it on your calendar, and just do it.

• **Take care of yourself first.** Chances are you attend to a lot of people each day: your students, colleagues, children, friends, and partner. Remember, if your own basic needs are not being met, if you are tired, hungry, lethargic, lonely, or uninspired, then there is a very good chance that you are not as good a caregiver as you could be. Once you are more healthy and balanced, you will have the physical, intellectual, and emotional energy needed to be a great friend, parent, lover, and, yes, teacher. Take care of yourself first!

Finally, I have a request. A danger when one writes a book about a particular subject is that people (including the author himself) begin to see you as an expert on that subject. Although that opinion may be warranted in some instances, it could not be further from the truth in this case. The more I read and the more I talk with teachers, the more I realize I still have a lot to learn about becoming a healthy and well-balanced teacher.

So here is the request: please share your ideas, questions, and strategies with me! I would love to hear from you to find out what you think about this topic. What ideas from this book resonated with you? What did I miss? What have you tried that was either a success or a flop? Send me an e-mail at wellbalancedteacher@gmail.com, and let me know what you're thinking. I promise to get back to you—that is, right after I come in from working in the garden or playing with my kids. I need to take care of myself first, after all!

References

Anderson, N. (2009, November 20). Gates Foundation gives $335 million to raise teacher effectiveness. *The Washington Post.* Retrieved March 2, 2010, from http://www.washingtonpost.com/wp-dyn/content/article/2009/11/19/AR2009111902211.html.

Antoniou, A. S., Polychroni, F., & Walters, B. (2000, July). *Sources of stress and professional burnout of teachers of special education needs in Greece.* Paper presented at ISEC 2000. Retrieved March 2, 2010, from http://www.isec2000.org.uk/abstracts/papers_p/polychroni_1.htm

Baker, M. (2004, March 27). Is teaching the most stressful job? Retrieved March 2, 2010, from http://news.bbc.co.uk/2/hi/uk_news/education/3573075.stm.

Barth, R. (2006, March). Improving relationships within the schoolhouse. *Educational Leadership, 63*(6), 8–13.

Block, S. (2003, October). Stressed out in the classroom. *American School Board Journal, 190*(10), 36–38.

Breus, M. J. (2006, March 15). Sleep habits: More important than you think: Chronic sleep deprivation may harm health. Retrieved December 21, 2009, from http://www.webmd.com/sleep-disorders/guide/important-sleep-habits.

Brown, E. (2009, September 3). School finds strength in "family." *The Washington Post.* Retrieved March 2, 2010, from http://www.washingtonpost.com/wp-dyn/content/article/2009/09/01/AR2009090103992.html.

Buck, P. (n.d.). Retrieved December 16, 2009, from http://www.quotationspage.com/quote/1780.htm.

Bushaw, W. J., & McNee, J. A. (2009, September). Americans speak out: Are educators listening? The 41st annual Phi Delta Kappa/Gallup Poll of the public's attitudes toward the public schools. *Phi Delta Kappan, 91*(1), 22.

Centers for Disease Control and Prevention. (2006, September 28). *Helicobacter pylori* and peptic ulcer disease: Myths. Retrieved March 2, 2010, from http://www.cdc.gov/ulcer/myth.htm.

Charney, R. (2002). *Teaching children to care: Classroom management for ethical and academic growth, K–8.* Greenfield, MA: Northeast Foundation for Children.

Clayton, M., & Forton, M. B. (2001). *Classroom spaces that work.* Greenfield, MA: Northeast Foundation for Children.

Cornforth, T. (2009, November 4). Urinary tract infections: Causes, symptoms, treatments. Retrieved March 2, 2010, from http://womenshealth.about.com/cs/bladderhealth/a/UTI.htm.

Danielson, C. (1996). *Enhancing professional practice.* Alexandria, VA: ASCD.

Educational Leadership. (December 2009/January 2010). Health and learning. (Entire issue.)

Graves, D. (2006). *A sea of faces: The importance of knowing your students.* Portsmouth, NH: Heinemann.

Green, L. (2009, December 16). Teachers might cut extra hours to protest policy. *Palm Beach Post News.* Retrieved March 2, 2010, from http://www.palmbeachpost.com/news/schools/teachers-might-cut-extra-hours-to-protest-policy-70409.html.

Hakanen, J. J., Bakker, A. B., & Schaufeli, W. B. (2006, January). Burnout and work engagement among teachers. *Journal of School Psychology, 60*(6), 495–513.

Houghton, P. (2001). Finding allies: Sustaining teachers' health and well-being. *Phi Delta Kappan, 82*(9), 706–711.

Ingebretsen, M. (2005, February 17). Organizational restructuring, employee stress and health. Retrieved March 2, 2010, from http://www.medpagetoday.com/Psychiatry/AnxietyStress/532.

Kohn, A. (1993). *Punished by rewards: The trouble with gold stars, incentive plans, A's, praise, and other bribes.* New York: Houghton Mifflin.

Louv, R. (2005). *Last child in the woods: Saving our children from nature-deficit disorder.* Chapel Hill, NC: Algonquin Books.

Maslow, A. H. (1943). A theory of human motivation. *Psychological Review, 50*(4), 370–396.

Mawhinney, L. (2008, June). Laugh so you don't cry: Teachers combating isolation in schools through humor and social support. *Ethnography and Education, 3*(2), 195–209.

Maxfield, D. (2009, October 7). Running into the fire. *Education Week.* Retrieved March 2, 2010, from http://www.edweek.org/ew/articles/2009/10/07/06maxfield.h29.html?r=1262527398

Newkirk, T. (2009, October 16). Stress, control, and the deprofessionalizing of teaching. *Education Week.* Retrieved March 2, 2010, from http://www.edweek.org/ew/articles/2009/10/21/08newkirk.h29.html?r=1701349221.

Pearson, C. L., & Moomaw, W. (2005). The relationship between teacher autonomy and work satisfaction, empowerment, and professionalism. *Educational Research Quarterly, 29*(1), 38–54.

Rodgers, R. (2007). Benefits of adequate hydration are mind boggling. Retrieved March 1, 2010, from http://ezinearticles.com/?Benefits-Of-Adequate-Hydration-Are-Mind-Boggling&id=899372.

Smith, M., Jaffe-Gill, E., & Segal, J. (2009, July). Understanding stress: Signs, symptoms, causes, and effects. Retrieved December 16, 2009, from http://www.helpguide.org/mental/stress_signs.htm.

Smith, M., Kemp, G., & Segal, J. (2009, May). Laughter is the best medicine: The health benefits of humor and laughter. Retrieved March 2, 2010, from http://helpguide.org/life/humor_laughter_health.htm.

Sorenson, R. D. (2007). Stress management in education: Warning signs and coping mechanisms. *British Educational Leadership, Management & Administration Society, 21*(3), 10.

Tschannen-Moran, M., & Woolfolk, A. (2001). Teacher efficacy: Capturing an elusive construct. *Teaching and Teacher Education, 17*(7), 783–805.

Van Der Linde, C. H. (2000, Winter). The teacher's stress and its implications for the school as an organization: How can TQM help? Retrieved December 16, 2009, from http://findarticles.com/p/articles/mi_qa3673/is_2_121/?tag=content;col1.

Zaslow, J. (2007, May). A new "greatest" generation. *The Week, 7*(309), 44–45.

Index

Page numbers followed by *f* denote figures.

About the Author

 Mike Anderson is a professional development specialist and consulting teacher for Northeast Foundation for Children, a nonprofit organization that supports teachers across the United States in implementing *Responsive Classroom* teaching practices. He taught 3rd, 4th, and 5th grades in public schools in New Hampshire and Connecticut for 15 years. He has also taught in preschools, coached swim teams, and taught graduate classes at the University of New Hampshire summer literacy institute. In 2004, he was awarded a national Milken Educator Award for excellence in teaching, and he was a finalist for New Hampshire Teacher of the Year in 2005. He is also the author of *The Research-Ready Classroom* (with Andy Dousis, Heinemann, 2006). Mike lives in Durham, New Hampshire, with his wife, Heather, and their two children, Ethan and Carly.

Related ASCD Resources: The Well-Balanced Teacher

At the time of publication, the following ASCD resources were available; for the most up-to-date information about ASCD resources, go to www.ascd.org. ASCD stock numbers are noted in parentheses.

Print Products

Creating a Healthy School Using the Healthy School Report Card: An ASCD Action Tool by David K. Lohrmann, Theresa Lewallen, and Pamela Karwasinski (#705191)

Educational Leadership, September 2005, The Whole Child (#106036)

Educational Leadership, December 2009 / January 2010, Health and Learning (#110023)

Keeping the Whole Child Healthy and Safe: Reflections on Best Practices in Learning, Teaching, and Leadership [E-BOOK] Edited by Marge Scherer (#110130)

THE WHOLE CHILD The Whole Child Initiative helps schools and communities create learning environments that allow students to be healthy, safe, engaged, supported, and challenged. To learn more about other books and resources that relate to the whole child, visit www.wholechildeducation.org.

For additional resources, visit us on the World Wide Web (http://www.ascd.org), send an e-mail message to member@ascd.org, call the ASCD Service Center (1-800-933-ASCD or 703-578-9600, then press 2), send a fax to 703-575-5400, or write to Information Services, ASCD, 1703 N. Beauregard St., Alexandria, VA 22311-1714 USA.